and Jerome Rothenberg

André Breton: Selections. Edited and with an Introduction by Mark Polizzotti

María Sabina: Selections. Edited by Jerome Rothenberg, with Texts and Commentaries by Álvaro Estrada and Others

* collage
* automatic writing
  (spoken thought) ─▷ _The Magnetic Fields_
* sleeping <u>fits</u>
* complete nonconformism

*The publisher gratefully acknowledges the generous contribution
to this book provided by the General Endowment Fund
of the Associates of the University of California Press.*

ANDRÉ BRETON: SELECTIONS

SELECTIONS

ANDRÉ BRETON

EDITED AND WITH AN INTRODUCTION BY

MARK POLIZZOTTI

UNIVERSITY OF CALIFORNIA PRESS

Berkeley Los Angeles London

All images courtesy Mark Polizzotti
unless otherwise noted.

University of California Press
Berkeley and Los Angeles, California

University of California Press, Ltd.
London, England

Library of Congress Cataloging-in-Publication Data
Breton, André, 1896–1966.
[Poems. English. Selections]
André Breton : Selections / André Breton ;
edited and with an introduction by Mark Polizzotti.
p. cm. — (Poets for the millennium ; 1)
Includes bibliographical references.
ISBN 0-520-23584-3 (alk. paper) — ISBN 0-520-23954-7 (alk. paper)
1. Breton, André, 1896–1966—Translations into English.
I. Polizzotti, Mark. II. Title. III. Series.
PQ2603.R35A27 2003
841'.912—dc21 2003041009

FRONTISPIECE: René Char, Georges Sadoul,
André Breton, and Paul Eluard clowning in a
Paris photo booth, ca. 1930. Courtesy Timothy Baum.

SADI, ALWAYS

CONTENTS

DOCUMENTS

INTRODUCTION *Phrases Knocking at the Window*

Theorist, polemicist, art critic, political agitator, Surrealist impresario, cultural terrorist: André Breton's public persona commands such dramatic attention that we might sometimes forget he was, first and foremost, a poet. And as these activities help define the man, his poems provide a remarkably faithful, if cryptic, record of his life. At the same time, these poems challenge our notions of autobiography—veering, sometimes in the course of a single work, from the pointedly candid to the maddeningly opaque. It is this mixture of transparency and obfuscation that underlies both the seduction and the frustration of Breton's poetical writings. In them, he rarely speaks directly of his concerns, whether philosophy, politics, emotional turbulence and group dynamics, admired predecessors, or valued contemporaries. Rather, he uses these concerns as conduits, means to channel the marvelous reality hidden just beneath the surface of our humdrum world.

The intricate collage of Breton's poetry begins, as if following a classical apprenticeship, with the imitation of his predecessors. His earliest pieces were wittingly obscure sonnets styled after the nineteenth-century Symbolists, whose verses he discovered in his early teens. It was from the Symbolists, with their penchant for abstruse formulations and sensual decadence (best visualized in the paintings of Gustave Moreau, another enthusiasm of Breton's during this time), that the young man early on adopted a taste for hermeticism that never entirely left his writing. He absorbed the precious aestheticism of such now-forgotten writers as René Ghil and Stuart Merrill, the dark and fusty enigmas of Villiers de l'Isle-Adam and Jean Lorrain. He became a passionate devotee of Stéphane Mallarmé, perhaps the most arcane poet France had yet produced, whom the young Breton considered "God made manifest."[1] And at almost the same time, he was enthralled by the liberating insouciance and perpetual adolescent revolt emanating from another literary deity, Arthur Rimbaud, "a veritable god of puberty such as no mythology had ever seen."[2]

Throughout his adult life, what interested Breton was less an author's work per se than the "human attitude" behind it. As he later put it, "Poetry, which is all I have ever appreciated in literature, emanates more from the lives of human beings—whether writers or not—than from what they have written or from what we might imagine they could write." Poetry, in other words, was primarily a means of accepting "the unacceptable human condition,"[3] a "specific solution to the problem of our lives."[4] More generally, poetry was a crystallization of Breton's belief that words and language could change the world, that they could act as passageways to a richer, more fulfilling universe, and even as tools for creating such a universe out of one's inner resources.

Finding a solution to "the problem of our lives" was not merely theoretical: in a very real sense, and from the beginning, poetry represented for Breton an alternative to a childhood he always remembered as sad, lonely, and bleak. Born on 19 February 1896, in the town of Tinchebray (Normandy), he spent his first four years surrounded by the wondrous Norman forests, but he grew up in the industrial Paris suburb of Pantin, under the care of his blandly ineffectual father and loveless, socially ambitious mother. Anxious that the boy make something of himself for the family's sake and ill satisfied with the rude en-

Bad Parents

vironment of Pantin, Marguerite Breton forbade her son from playing with the neighborhood's working-class children or exploring his budding interest in literature, which was in her eyes a waste of time that only distracted Breton from his studies. Breton's later celebration of childhood memories as "the most fertile that exists" and his judgment that the "unintegrated" feeling of childhood "comes closest to one's 'real life'"[5] are in this light a wistful commentary on an existence he never knew—or perhaps on the lost paradise of his Norman infancy.

Little wonder, then, that Breton's demands of poetry often contained a pronounced element of escapism, for literature was often his only path away from his mother's strictures and his depressing surroundings. He described these demands in a revealing passage from 1923:

> The only thing I would consider worth doing is escaping, as much as possible, from that human type we all share in. For me, to get away from the psychological rule, to no matter how small a degree, is equivalent to inventing new ways of feeling. Even with all the disappointments it has already caused me, I still see poetry as the terrain on which the terrible difficulties that consciousness has with confidence, in a given individual, have the best chance of being resolved. That is why I occasionally act so harshly toward it, why I can forgive it no abdication.[6]

As a child, he had been particularly enchanted by the macabre Celtic folk tales told by his Norman grandfather, and later by adventure novels such as Louis de Bellemare's *Costal l'Indien,* with its fabulous Mexican setting. As a teenager, his passion for the Symbolists largely hinged on their ability to evoke a misty, mysterious world so different from the industrial drabness of Pantin. Later, as an adult, his taste ran toward the fanciful flights of Rimbaud's "The Drunken Boat," the amoral hallucinations of Lautréamont's *Maldoror,* the exotic locales parading through Apollinaire's "Zone," and the absinthe-soaked deliria of Alfred Jarry's *Ubu* plays. Similarly, his own poems, whether dredged raw from his unconscious or based on a very deliberate appreciation of his environment, generally followed the prescription he first sketched at age seventeen: that the true merit of poetry is to "unsettle the walls of the real that enclose us."[7] It is appropriate that Breton's first known poem, published under a pseudonym when he was sixteen, was a hymn to that other great means of escape, the dream:

A dream is a gaze cast unendingly far …
Something that's blue, like a fragment of myth …
A glittering jewel, but tarnished by day …
Perhaps the sole fruit that our daylight permits … […][8]

In the fall of 1913, under parental pressure, Breton enrolled in medical school—though, as he said, his "physical presence on the lecture-hall benches or at the laboratory tables should not imply the same presence of mind."[9] Instead, he pursued his literary activities as chances allowed, publishing three poems the following spring in the Symbolist magazine *La Phalange* and making the acquaintance of Symbolism's leading survivor, Paul Valéry. Breton's poems from this time show distinct traces of Valéry's influence, with their convoluted phrasings and muted eroticism (even if the nymph of "Merry"—a prime example—has more in common with Maxfield Parrish than with Moreau's *Delilah*). Still, it was not so much Valéry's poetic credentials that appealed to Breton, nor even that he had once frequented the revered Mallarmé, but his cerebral narrative *An Evening with Monsieur Teste*— and, even more so, the fact that in 1896 *Teste* had acted as Valéry's farewell to published literature. "In my eyes," Breton later told an interviewer, Valéry "benefited from the prestige inherent in a myth …

that of a man turning his back on his life's work one fine day, as if, once he had reached certain heights, the work somehow 'rejected' its creator."[10] When Valéry later broke his twenty-year silence with the epic poem *The Young Fate,* Breton felt personally betrayed.

Shortly before his nineteenth birthday, in February 1915, Breton was drafted into the Great War, "a cesspool of blood, mud, and idiocy,"[11] which soon had him putting his scant medical training to work as an orderly in the city of Nantes. The makeshift wards afforded him his first direct contact with the mysteries of the unconscious, partly

Breton as a medical student, ca. 1913.

through his treatment of shell-shocked patients—victims of what today would be called post-traumatic stress disorder, in most cases suffering not so much from clinical delusions as from the technological horrors into which their CO's had thrust them—and partly through his discovery of Freud, who was all but unknown in France at the time. Although Breton continued to write, he considered abandoning literature to become a practicing psychiatrist. The two were not so contradictory as it might seem, for Breton's interest in his patients focused on how they presented verbally more than medically. "Nothing affects me so much as interpreting these madmen," he told a correspondent. "My fate, instinctively, is to subject the artist to a similar test."[12] For Breton, the genius of these "madmen" (regardless of whether or not they were actually mad) lay in their instinctive ability to fashion "the most distant relations between ideas, the rarest verbal

Marguerite and Louis Breton later in life. *Courtesy Sylvie Sator.*

alliances"[13]—in other words, to create poetry of the most startling, un-
usual, and fertile kind. Indeed, it is doubtful that Breton the grudging
intern did much to help his patients. A writer above all, he took from
his consultations and his readings of the early psychoanalytic theorists
the inspiration for his later soundings of the unconscious mind. The
prose monologue "Subject," written during that period, is an attempt

to capture the logic and language of one particular patient, who claimed that the war was but a vast simulacrum staged for his sole benefit. In 1930, Breton would further push his attempts to recreate from within the so-called psychotic discourse in *The Immaculate Conception,* whose centerpiece is various "simulations" of mental illnesses.

During these years as well, Breton met the young men who would form the core of the early Surrealist group—Louis Aragon, Philippe Soupault, and Paul Eluard, all fledgling poets like himself—along with others whose example would largely shape this period of his life: most notably the poet, critic, and impresario Guillaume Apollinaire and a twenty-year-old grenadier corporal named Jacques Vaché. From Apollinaire, Breton learned the habit of café meetings, the omnivorous interest in all forms of the unusual. But it was the sardonic Vaché, with his dismissive concept of *umor* ("a sense of the theatrical—and joyless—pointlessness of everything"[14]) and his disdain of Breton's beloved literature, who exerted the most profound and lasting influence.

The two men met in early 1916 during Breton's rounds in the military hospital, where Vaché was recuperating from a leg wound, and where he spent his time sketching a series of curious postcards depicting elegantly aloof men (usually himself) standing amidst the war's carnage as if against the zinc of a fashionable bar. He wove around himself a dramatic cloak of elaborate lies that he did not bother to maintain from one day to the next; his past, to hear him tell it, was exotic and alluringly unfathomable. Once released, Vaché spent his days on the waterfront of Nantes and his evenings around town in various military costumes, dreaming of a composite uniform that could be mistaken simultaneously for that of the Allies and that of the enemy, for the war was a particular target of his sarcasm ("My God, it's hot—

Jacques Vaché in uniform, around the time of
his meeting with Breton. *Courtesy Georges Sebbag.*

(Vaché)

I'll never win all these wars!!!"[15]). With Breton, he flitted from cin-
ema to cinema, rarely staying in place for more than five minutes,
pasting together a collage of unrelated sequences more interesting
than any of the individual films, or setting up a noisy picnic in the
seats, to the astonishment and outrage of the movie audience. At one
theatrical premiere, he showed up waving a pistol, grumbling that he

wanted to shoot the spectators because he didn't like the stage sets. "I have never experienced anything quite as *magnetizing,*" Breton later wrote. "The important thing is that we came out of it 'charged' for a few days."[16]

Such moments can easily be dismissed as at best adolescent pranks, at worst acts of potentially criminal negligence. What does bear noting is the lasting impact they had on Breton's psychology, attitudes, and writing. At the time, he summed up Vaché's influence as one of deterrence: "If not for him, I might have become a poet. He overcame in me the conspiracy of dark forces that makes one believe he can have anything as absurd as a vocation."[17] The elegiac bravado begs the obvious fact that Breton did write poems, then and later. Instead of continuing to emulate Mallarmé and his followers, however, he began producing work that reflected the disorientation of his relationship with his new friend, and that pointed toward a much less traveled course in the years ahead.

Compare pieces such as "Black Forest," "For Lafcadio," and "Mister V," all written in the spring of 1918, with a predecessor such as "Age" from two years before. Each of these works is based on an autobiographical moment: "Age" is a Rimbaldian meditation on turning twenty, "Black Forest" and "For Lafcadio" interweave snippets of Breton's literary passions (Rimbaud's legendary break-up with Verlaine for the first, André Gide's casually homicidal antihero for the second), while "Mister V" pieces together fragments of the author's relations with Paul Valéry, including excerpts from the mentor's correspondence. But in structure and conception, the approach of the latter three works could not be more different from the *Illuminations*-derived prose of "Age" or the formal versifying of earlier works such as "Merry." Here, blanks speak louder than the words punctuating them, and the words themselves are only cryptic snatches, half-erased ciphers that add up to an intangible sum. "I managed to extract from the blank lines of [these poems] an incredible advantage," Breton later explained:

> These lines were the closed eye to the operations of thought that I believed I was obliged to keep hidden from the reader ... I had begun to cherish words excessively for the space they allow around them, for their tangencies with countless other words that I did not utter. The poem BLACK FOREST derives precisely from this state of mind. It took me six months to write it, and you may take my word for it that I did not rest a single day.[18]

If there is one overriding aesthetic of this period, it is the collage, an assemblage of "indirect loans," disparate fragments borrowed from life, literature, advertising slogans, and any other element deemed useful. Apollinaire had experimented with this approach in his "conversation poems," fashioned from bits of overheard small talk. The Cubist painters had tried it in the visual domain. In his 1918 trilogy of poems, Breton uses the minutiae of admired literary figures as signposts, guides for the text, even as accomplices—just as he named his friends in many of his prose writings throughout his life. Even Breton's daily existence at this time was a collage, a sundry patchwork of military duties, long-distance literary activities, periodic exchanges with his friends Aragon and Soupault, and, more than anything, his infrequent but much-awaited encounters with Vaché, who was now back on the frontlines.

For Breton, meeting Vaché had entailed a radical revision of everything he'd been taught, not only by family and society, but even by his supposedly advanced literary heroes. Not surprisingly, it also entailed a revision of his poetic forms. Indeed, although "Mister V" is by Breton's own admission based on his waning relations with Valéry, whose irritating paternalism and unseasonable good sense seep between the lines of the poem, behind Valéry, as in all the blanks from this trilogy of 1918, one can also glimpse the elusive figure of Mister Vaché, with his frequent absences, his flippant and caustic rejection of art ("ART IS FOLLY"), his mysterious past full of gaps and silences, and the disjunctions and disruptions that his sporadic presence occasioned in Breton's life.

As the war slowly progressed, Breton's meetings with Vaché took on an increasingly somber cast. Vaché, Breton told a correspondent in 1917, was playing "that victim of modern inevitability: the traveler. One of his great roles ... Dryness of heart; nonetheless allow for friendship."[19] The following spring, the traveler himself was exercising his sarcasm on Breton: "Everything is so amusing—very amusing, it's a fact—how amusing life is!—(and what if one killed oneself as well, instead of just going away?)."[20] In the end, the remark proved to be less casual than it appeared, or even than Vaché might have intended. Shortly after the Armistice, Breton made plans to rejoin his friend, appropriately via a collage-letter, but the message never reached its destination: on 6 January 1919, having taken a hotel room with several army buddies, Vaché stripped naked, swallowed an overdose of opium pellets, and did not wake up. The wound was one from which Breton never recovered, and for years afterward many of his writings carried traces of Vaché's final disappearance. "I cannot express here the pain that the news of his death caused me, or the trouble I had getting over it," he wrote in 1921. "For a long time, Jacques Vaché was everything in the world to me."[21]

Eager to fill the void, Breton sought replacements for his departed comrade in various surrogates, and nowhere more so than in the charismatic spokesman of the Zurich Dada movement, the Rumanian-born poet Tristan Tzara. Breton knew Tzara, who was then in

Louis Aragon, ca. 1920.

Switzerland, only from his writings and others' reports, but this did not deter him from projecting enormous expectations on the man. "If I have an insane confidence in you, it's because you remind me of a friend, my best friend, Jacques Vaché, who died several months ago," he wrote to the Dadaist in April 1919.[22]

When Tzara finally left Zurich for Paris in January 1920, largely at Breton's urging, the future Surrealists threw themselves wholeheartedly into Dada's infiltration of the French capital. "There were several of us who awaited Tzara in Paris as if he were that savage adolescent [Rimbaud] who fell upon the devastated capital at the time of the Commune," Aragon later remarked.[23] Disgusted with the French literary scene and with the postwar atmosphere in general, Breton, Aragon, Eluard, Soupault, and others around them enthusiastically welcomed Dada's flamboyant refusal of everything that constituted good breeding, good values, or good sense. For the next two years, they participated in Dada "demonstrations": theatrical performances featuring nonsense readings, disturbing noises, harangues to the crowd—anything to rile the audience, to remind it of how furious the younger generation was about the war, how much they loathed the writers and artists who had pamphleteered for it and the culture that had spawned it. "The beginnings of Dada were not the beginnings of an art, but those of a disgust," Tzara wrote. "Disgust with the magnificence of philosophers who for three thousand years have been explaining everything to us."[24]

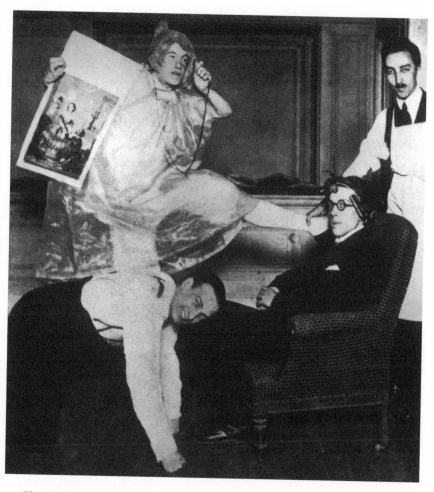

Eluard, Philippe Soupault (on the floor), Breton (with revolvers strapped to his head), and Théodore Fraenkel performing *You'll Forget Me* at the Salle Gaveau, May 1920.

hahahaha - just some young intellectuals having fun

Breton's work from this period is a suicidal pact with itself, an erasure of his own past and an embrace of Dada's across-the-board demolition. One poem, "Counterfeit Coin," stretches a self-serious stanza of his from 1914 into a broad burlesque, while another, "PSST," turns his byline into just another "Breton" listing in the Paris phone book, amid dairymen and coal merchants (giving a new twist to Rimbaud's famous dictum, "the writer's hand is no better than the ploughman's"). In a play written with Soupault at around the same time, Breton even thought momentarily to take Dada's self-destructive nihilism a step further, by ending the last act of the (presumably) single performance with a literal bullet to the head onstage.

The real revolution of this period, however, ultimately had little to do with Dada, or with any of Breton's previous literary models. In the spring of 1919, before Dada came to Paris, and just as his first book of poems, *Pawnshop* (*Mont de piété*), was coming off press, Breton turned back to his psychiatric studies and to the startling imagery that he'd heard from his traumatized patients during the war. This imagery, as he described it a few years later, at first occurred to him largely unbidden:

> One evening ... before I fell asleep, I perceived, so clearly articulated that it was impossible to change a word, but nonetheless removed from the sound of any voice, a rather strange phrase which came to me without any apparent relationship to the events in which, my consciousness agrees, I was then involved, a phrase which seemed to me insistent, a phrase, if I may be so bold, *which was knocking at the window.* I took cursory note of it and prepared to move on when its organic character caught my attention ... I realized that I was dealing with an image of a fairly rare sort, and all I could think of was to incorporate it into my material for poetic construction ... I resolved to obtain from myself what we were trying to obtain from [my patients], namely, a monologue spoken as rapidly as possible without any intervention on the

part of the critical faculties, a monologue consequently unencumbered by the slightest inhibition and which was, as closely as possible, akin to *spoken thought*.[25]

That June, while awaiting his discharge from the army, Breton spent hours in his hotel room with Soupault, "blackening" sheets of paper with a rapid flow of words jotted down without premeditation or vigilance—words that, he hoped, would form a verbal record of his unconscious. The resulting book, *The Magnetic Fields* (*Les Champs magnétiques*), stands as the first full volume of "automatic writing" and inaugurated a decade of experimentation with coaxing the "mouth of shadows" (as Victor Hugo had called it) to speak. Though eventually abandoned and much maligned, even by its champion, this writing was the cornerstone on which Surrealism was built.

The response to *The Magnetic Fields* was not entirely what Breton had hoped. Immediately after its publication in the spring of 1920, he sent a copy to Sigmund Freud in Vienna, expecting the father of psychoanalysis to recognize in it an unprecedentedly fertile ground for examination. But Freud, like any detective, was more interested in normalcy and its discontents than in the unconscious ostensibly laid bare, and his bland and bemused reply to the young French poet was a harsh disappointment. (Or perhaps Freud recognized that the author had made slight edits to the text before publication, further undermining its value as a psychoanalytic tool.) Nor did the book receive much credit on the literary level: despite Breton's anticipation of a major reaction from the critics—if not acclaim, then at least some satisfying uproar—it went politely unnoticed at home as well.

Despite this setback, over the next two years Breton sought out manifestations of the unconscious in everyday life, both through written automatism and through such extra-literary essays as "sleeping fits," séances in which certain members of the group began reciting

fabulous impromptu stories while in a sleep-like trance. One partici-
pant, the poet Robert Desnos, proved especially adept at these, and
even began improvising complex puns that he claimed derived from
his telepathic communication with Marcel Duchamp in New York.
(Duchamp, via his alter ego "Rrose Sélavy," had recently begun in-
scribing such wordplay on his visual works.) Even the odd daily oc-
currence could provide a flash of the unknown: Breton's article "The
New Spirit" from 1922 describes a chance encounter individually ex-
perienced by the author and two of his friends and above all shows the
significance with which he invested such fortuitous juxtapositions.

By 1924, a considerable group was forming around Breton, which over
the next five years would include some of his generation's most inno-
vative and rebellious minds: his old friends Soupault, Aragon, and
Eluard, as well as the writers Desnos, Benjamin Péret, Roger Vitrac,
Jacques Prévert, Michel Leiris, Raymond Queneau, Georges Bataille,
Antonin Artaud, and René Crevel; the artists Max Ernst, Joan Miró,
Yves Tanguy, André Masson, Man Ray, Salvador Dalí, and Alberto
Giacometti; the filmmaker Luis Buñuel; and many others whose
names are less familiar. (Others still, such as Picasso and the resolutely
independent Duchamp, maintained a lifelong contact with Breton
and occasionally participated in Surrealist exhibitions, but they were
never part of the group proper.) What held these disparate elements
together was Breton's personal magnetism. Notoriously charismatic,
he had a remarkable talent to inspire friendships in others that Desnos
described as "one of the moral honors of our time." Some of these
figures later recalled the extraordinary attention Breton could pay to
those who interested him, his ability to *listen* like no one else. The
group "loved Breton like a woman," Jacques Prévert said, and the his-
torian Maurice Nadeau remarked that "those who enjoyed the mo-

At the amusement park, early 1920s. Max Morise is at the wheel, followed by Eluard, Simone Breton, Joseph Delteil, Gala Eluard, Robert Desnos, and Breton, with Max Ernst on the bicycle.

ments of his unforgettable friendship ... were ready to sacrifice everything to him: wives, mistresses, friends."[26] This charisma helps explain why so many—wives, mistresses, friends—remained with Breton through some equally unforgettable moments of boorishness and disregard.

One who had recently received a taste of this disregard was Breton's former comrade-in-Dada Tristan Tzara. Although Breton had championed the advent of Dada in 1920 and proselytized for the movement, before long he found himself profoundly disillusioned by the pointless repetitiveness of its manifestations, the "pitiful carnival ruses"[27] Tzara used to attract the public time after time after time. In 1922, during a failed bid to organize his own "International Congress for the Determination and Defense of the Modern Spirit," Breton dismissed the foreign-born poet as a "a publicity-mongering impostor ... a person known as the promoter of a 'movement' that comes from Zurich"[28]—a hint of xenophobia that lost him credit with many of the cosmopolitan writers he sought to attract as allies. The following year, he and his supporters leapt onstage to disrupt the single performance of Tzara's play *The Gas Heart*. In the ensuing brawl, sets and costumes were destroyed, Breton fractured one actor's arm with his walking stick, and the frantic Tzara was finally forced to call in the police—a tactical error of his own, given the mostly anti-establishment audience, that Breton was still exploiting years afterward. By the time of the Surrealist group's formation in 1924, no warmth was left between Breton and the man in whom he had once professed "insane confidence" (although, in a gauge of Surrealism's ever-revolving membership, Tzara would briefly return to the fold in 1930).

Building on the shared practice of automatic writing, which the group around Breton had dubbed "Surrealism" after a coinage of Apollinaire's, Breton decided to publish a collection of automatic prose poems, more extensive than *The Magnetic Fields,* that would illustrate the concept and importance of psychic automatism. The pieces, written in the spring of 1924, were grouped together under the title *Soluble Fish* (*Poisson soluble*), to which he thought to add a theoretical preface, hoping to forestall the lack of interest that had greeted *The Magnetic Fields* four years earlier. Ultimately, it was a case of the tail wagging the fish (as the critic Susan Suleiman put it): the preface took predominance, even as the prose poems were pared down by two-thirds, and the book was published in October as the *Manifesto of Surrealism.*

The *Manifesto* is a brilliantly worded, carefully *reasoned* tract on the primacy of irrational thought. It is also a rallying cry and statement of purpose: "Surrealism, such as I conceive of it, asserts our complete *nonconformism,*" Breton stated,[29] warning that it "does not allow those who devote themselves to it to forsake it whenever they like. There is every reason to maintain that it acts on the mind very much as drugs do; like drugs, it creates a certain state of need and can push man to frightful revolts."[30] And, as much as anything, the *Manifesto* is one of the most masterful self-advertisements of twentieth-century literature. This is not accidental: at the time it was written, Breton's group was in competition with the poet Ivan Goll, a devoted follower of Apollinaire, for moral ownership of the term "Surrealism" (which Goll meant to preserve as Apollinaire had originally used it). After several months of dueling it out in the daily papers, reported with a fervency that American journalism normally reserves only for the sports columns, the antagonists raised the ante: Goll published the first, and only, issue of his magazine *Surréalisme;* Breton countered with the one-two punch of his own magazine, *La Révolution surréaliste* (which lasted for five years and spawned numerous others), and the *Manifesto of Surrealism.* Breton knew his audience. Next to the boldness of *La Révolution surréaliste*—the magazine's signature orange-red cover was programmatic—and the aggressive freshness of the *Manifesto,* Goll looked exactly like what he was: a pale imitator of yesterday's heroes. His claim ended then and there.

This is not to diminish the genuine import of the *Manifesto* as a philosophical statement. Breton might pack the text with tongue-in-cheek recipes for using Surrealism "to catch the eye of a woman you pass in the street" and "against death," or with his famous mock-dictionary definition:

> SURREALISM, n. Psychic automatism in its pure state, by which one proposes to express—verbally, by means of the written word, or in any other manner—the actual functioning of thought. Dictated by thought, in the absence of any control exercised by reason, exempt from any aesthetic or moral concern.[31]

But beneath this showmanship is a stirring call to the marvelous, in all its forms—"Let us not mince words: the marvelous is always beautiful, anything marvelous is beautiful, in fact only the marvelous is beautiful"[32]—and against "the absolute rationalism that is still in vogue."[33] It is a call to man, "that inveterate dreamer," to reject the "lusterless fate" promised by centuries of Greco-Latin logic. Almost a century later, vast stretches of the territory Breton maps out beckon just as magically as they did, at least for some, in 1920s Paris.

Finally, the *Manifesto* is a summation and definition of the Surrealist movement in its first phase and of Breton's poetics up to that time. The hundred-odd pages of *Soluble Fish,* included as an appendix, illustrate the depths of the unconscious reservoir (just as Breton's second poetry collection, *Earthlight* [*Clair de terre*], published in 1923, showcased his automatic verse from the previous three years), while the sheer brashness of the text itself is an alias for the aggressive iconoclasm of Surrealism's external profile. Indeed, the group's first years were marked by willful controversy: its ostentatious hectoring of the literary establishment earned it the enmity of its peers, while its embrace of the newly formed French Communist Party tipped public disapproval into outrage. And we, as products of our blasé postmodern age, can only imagine the fury that greeted the collective broadside *A Corpse,* published to mock the death of the nationally beloved novelist Anatole France. Like the Surrealists' public stances—social, political, and artistic—it set the tone for a boisterous journey ahead.

During the height of his involvement in Dada, Breton had met and married Simone Kahn, the daughter of a comfortably middle-class Jewish family. By 1925, the marriage, to all appearances, retained a fair portion of complicity and friendship—Simone was one of the few women to take an active part (such as it was) in the Surrealist group—but little physical passion. Simone began pursuing a more independent life with her own friends, while Breton developed a violent crush on the poet and socialite Lise Meyer (who later published under the name Lise Deharme). In his autobiographical narrative *Nadja* (1928), Lise is the "lady of the gloves," whose first appearance so terrified him that he could not speak. More privately, she was "my lovely foreigner my loss of paradise"[34] in the letters and poems with which Breton petitioned her. "The event of our meeting," he complained in one, "was like the end of the world for me, while for you it was an insignificant happenstance."[35] Though Lise was flattered by the attentions of a rising young literary star and had nothing against a sporting flirtation, Breton's gravid nature was not to her taste, and his sexual longings went unrequited.

It was a different matter with Suzanne Muzard, a child, like Breton, of Paris's working-class suburbs, who entered his life in late 1927, just as Lise Meyer was exiting. "Tall, slender, gracefully shaped, with regular, slightly Nordic features," was how one Surrealist described her. "Very flirtatious and attractive, [she] loved love and luxury."[36] Within days of their meeting, Breton and Suzanne fled to the south of France, leaving behind both the patient Simone and Suzanne's live-in

Breton and Suzanne
Muzard, ca. 1931.

lover, the novelist Emmanuel Berl. The atmosphere of these escapades is captured—at least partly—in another unpublished poem, "Make it so daylight . . . ," written the following summer. But a more accurate picture is given in the final pages of *Nadja,* which evoke not only the mad passion but also the jealousies, recriminations, demands, and ultimately the incompatibility of the two lovers. For three years, Breton and Suzanne pursued a complicated tango of rupture and reconciliation, infidelity and betrayal, as she shuttled between the Surrealist and her earlier lover Berl. "Make it so daylight . . . ," composed in one of the couple's rare moments of harmony, is an intimate portrait of romantic love at its most ardent. To a large extent, however, the poem was also just wishful thinking.

In all this time, Simone had patiently weathered first her husband's infatuation with Lise, then his carnal involvement with Suzanne—both of which were dutifully reported to her by Breton himself. "Suzanne is utterly exquisite," he wrote her from a Toulon hotel during that first trip. "She has told me marvelous stories that I was born to hear and that you would love. Truly marvelous stories. Not for a moment has she been anything but what I imagined her to be . . . maybe a thousand times better. This is the first time in a week I've left her side for even ten minutes."[37] When Suzanne began pressuring Breton to divorce Simone and marry her instead, however, the situation rapidly deteriorated, and it turned definitively ugly after Breton, not immune to double standards, learned that Simone had been secretly conducting an affair of her own with a second-string Surrealist named Max Morise. Things turned uglier still in 1930, when Breton, finally through his bitter divorce, discovered that Suzanne had just married his rival Berl instead—which did not keep the two from maintaining their turbulent affair for over another year.

Breton's writings from this period reflect the black despair of his emotional trials. This despair shows in the tract *A suivre* (*To Be Continued*), a record of the group's widespread "excommunications" in the spring of 1929, which saw the acrimonious departures of Desnos, Soupault, Artaud, Bataille, Leiris, and a number of others. It shows in the bilious diatribes of the *Second Manifesto of Surrealism,* published later that year as an apologia for Surrealism's recent changes of course, notably its rejection of psychic automatism in favor of Communist politics and, more internally, its excoriation of some of its own members—including many of those Breton had trumpeted so highly in the first *Manifesto:*

> The lack of inhibition that we feel in appraising, from day to day, the
> degree of moral qualification of various people, the ease with which
> Surrealism, at the first sign of compromise, prides itself in bidding a
> fond farewell to this person or that, is less than ever to the liking of a
> few journalistic jerks, for whom the dignity of man is at the very most
> a subject for derisive laughter.... Why should we go on playing the
> role of those who are fed up and disgusted? A policeman, a few gay
> dogs, two or three pen pimps, several mentally unbalanced persons, a
> cretin ... is this not the making of an amusing, innocuous team, a faithful replica of life, a team of men paid piecework, winning on points?
> SHIT.[38]   *Haha!*

The despair also shows in the collaborative poem cycle *Ralentir travaux* (named after a common road sign meaning "slow down work ahead"), written with Paul Eluard and the Surrealist newcomer René Char during a car trip to Avignon in the spring of 1930, in which Breton's contributions speak of "women who in hate are taller and slimmer than praying mantises." An atmosphere of menace infuses these and other poems of the time, placing them along a line that stretches from the Gothic novel to such later American productions as W. S. Merwin's early poem "Caesar" and John Ashbery's "Forties Flick."

Perhaps this sense of danger stems from the fact that these works map a different, less familiar territory: no longer the life of the mind but of the heart—a heart, as Breton put it in one of his poems for Lise, "through which her heart has passed." Where poems such as "Sunflower" or "In the Eyes of the Gods" conjure self-generated landscapes populated by literary images, chance memories, and romantic objects that seem largely imaginary, those written in the time of Lise and Suzanne are centered almost obsessively on love experienced yet always beyond reach, for women who "smash the jewel of this day into a thousand shards." In few works is this more evident than "Free Union," a long litany of Suzanne's body in the style of the Renaissance *blason,* the serenity of courtly tradition replaced by the flashing turbulence of love shattered. "My wife whose hair is brush fire / Whose thoughts are summer lightning," Breton wrote in May 1931, shortly after he and Suzanne had parted for the final time.

"Free Union" was featured as one of the new poems in Breton's third collection, *The White-Haired Revolver* (*Le Revolver aux cheveux blancs*), published in 1932. The volume contained a number of the pieces he had written in the nine years since *Earthlight,* along with a selection of earlier work dating back to 1915. It is Breton's most accomplished book of poems, but overall the atmosphere emanating from it is one of sadness, as if everything had been cast into doubt.

While *Pawnshop* bespeaks a clever apprentice learning his chops and *Earthlight* a cocky and self-assured, if not wholly masterful, young poet reveling in his own discoveries, *The White-Haired Revolver* shows all the signs of mature disillusionment. This is the work of a man who had gone through a divorce and two painful separations and was doubting whether love would ever be his; who had assembled some of the most radical minds of his generation, only to have many of them fall away because of personal, political, or artistic incompatibility; who had seen his greatest hopes for a true revolution of the mind and of the human condition falter and snag on the persistent barbs of human failing.

Large among these disappointments was the ultimate inability of automatic writing to provide the kind of universal revelation and personal liberation Breton had once envisioned for it. "The history of automatic writing in Surrealism," he wrote in 1933, "is one of continual misfortune"—not least because of authorial vanity and "despicable poetic rivalries" on the part of those who practiced it.[39] While many of the poems in *The White-Haired Revolver* still show distinct traces of the automatic process, and while Breton would never entirely abandon it, one gets the sense that in this book, the "real life" he had earlier equated with access to unconscious strata was already being sought elsewhere.

Breton's emotional life as well seems to have pulled him away from his original poetic wellsprings. Even more than with the lines to Lise and Suzanne, his poetry at this time reflects a far greater share of outside reality—sometimes sounding very much like straightforward confessional poetry and sometimes coming dangerously close to what Breton himself dismissed as "circumstantial" or topical verse, poems written for a specific occasion or cause. His contribution in 1933 to the collective pamphlet *Violette Nozières,* in support of a girl indicted for her father's murder, hews closer to the lurid prose of tabloid headlines than to the lucid poetry of "spoken thought."

This is no less true, though perhaps less evident, in *The Air of Water* (*L'Air de l'eau*), a suite of poems written the following year to his second wife, Jacqueline Lamba. As famously described in his narrative *Mad Love* (*L'Amour fou*), Breton had first encountered Jacqueline in a Paris café, supposedly by chance, then spent the night walking with her through the central market of Les Halles. Several days later, a long-forgotten poem of his from 1923, "Sunflower," began pressing insistently at his consciousness, until Breton realized that the poem could be read line for line as a harbinger of this meeting. Every element of "Sunflower"—the farm imagery, the specifically named Paris settings—suddenly seemed to correspond to a nocturnal stroll that would not take place for another eleven years. By the time of *The Air of Water,* written only months after this stroll, the poetic prophecy of "Sunflower" had given way to a lyricized rendering of the facts. Automatism still inflects the verbal constructions, but overall these stanzas derive from a much more deliberate choice of images and incidents used to evoke the couple's first days together—from the "lovely half-light of 1934" to the "scream from the Maternity Hospital" near Jacqueline's apartment to the water motif, a reference to her job as an "undine," or underwater dancer.

But more than anything, it was the events of the outside world, notably Breton's political involvements, that proved inconducive to psychic automatism. Since the mid-1920s, Breton had been trying to make common cause with the French Communist Party (PCF), to find ways of reconciling the Communists' wage-and-labor platform with the Surrealists' program of dreams, mad love, and "freedom the color of man." The match was ill-conceived from the start and became more so with passing time. As the French Communists veered increasingly toward the hard-line Stalinism blowing in from the East, Breton's rigorous and very individual pursuit of the unconscious and of a personal romanticism only made him more suspect in their eyes. By the time of the Communist-sponsored Congress of Writers for the Defense of Culture of 1935, a vast undertaking involving prominent leftist writers from three continents, the Surrealists were viewed with such hostility that the organizers banned their participation outright. Enraged, Breton argued for inclusion, but the Soviet delegation dug in its heels. Only with the suicide of the Surrealist writer and PCF intimate René Crevel, who had labored desperately to bring the two sides together, did the Soviets relent—and, even then, the Surrealists were not given the stage until nearly midnight, after most of the audience had left.

In the wake of this final rejection, and with signs of increasing Soviet repression visible to anyone who chose to see, Breton turned definitively against Stalin and joined the Trotskyist opposition. In 1938, he and Jacqueline spent four months with Trotsky and the painters Diego Rivera and Frida Kahlo in Mexico, where Breton and the exiled Russian coauthored the "Manifesto for an Independent Revolutionary Art." When Breton returned to France later that summer, he also tried to establish a Trotskyist action committee and even began making some cursory inroads. But the outbreak of the Second World War the following September put an abrupt end to such activities. Eleven months later, Trotsky was assassinated, and the Stalinist line hardened still further.

With the political situation in such upheaval, it is not surprising that the mid- to late 1930s saw the scarcest poetic output of Breton's career, a comparative handful of published and unpublished poems. His writings from this time, in fact, consist mainly of polemical tracts, *Mad Love,* and the *Anthology of Black Humor (Anthologie de l'humour noir*), an edited collection of short writings by authors ranging from Swift to Dalí that he assembled in 1937. Based on and amplifying Jacques Vaché's notion of *umor,* what Breton called "black humor" seemed to capture perfectly the somber tone of those years. Black humor "is the mortal enemy of sentimentality," he wrote in the introduction, "a way of affirming, above and beyond 'the absolute revolt of adolescence and the internal revolt of adulthood,' a *superior revolt of the mind.*"[40] Breton himself stressed the timeliness of his anthology as the threat of war became imminent, telling a prospective publisher that it "would have a considerable *tonic* value"[41] if published then. (Whether or not he was correct will never be known: in a twist worthy of its subject, the book suffered numerous production delays and government censorship and, although printed in 1940, did not actually see the light of day until 1945.)

As for poetry, it was only after war was declared and Breton, following a brief tour as an army doctor, found himself in the Unoccupied Zone awaiting passage to America that he began to write it in earnest again. First came "Full Margin," composed in the summer of 1940 in Provence, where he was staying with his friend and doctor, Pierre Mabille. In it, Breton celebrated his intellectual guides (Hegel, Meister Eckhart, Novalis, Marat); various heretical figures from Church history (Joachim of Floris, Cornelis Jansen, Mother Angélique Arnauld); and his wife, Jacqueline—all in a seeming attempt to exorcise his anxieties about the fate of Europe, the rise of religious conservatism in Vichy France, and his fears for his and his family's safety. These fears were not illusory, for, as he later told an interviewer, the situation at the time was "extremely somber ... Certain courtesans of the new regime, moreover, even went so far as to accuse Surrealism in the press of having had a hand in the military defeat. The immediate prospects were quite alarming."[42]

Breton, André Masson, Jacqueline Breton, and Ernst
review emigration possibilities with Varian Fry, winter 1940.

The winter of 1940–1941 was spent with Jacqueline and their five-
year-old daughter, Aube, in Marseille, the jumping-off place for thou-
sands of hopeful émigrés. The Bretons stayed at the Villa Air-Bel, an
old mansion rented by the American-sponsored Emergency Rescue

Committee to house refugees in transit; as the family of a prominent leftist intellectual, they were among the few invited to share the spacious (and, all things considered, relatively luxurious) accommodations. Breton himself passed much of that December in the greenhouse on the vast Air-Bel property, creating the epic work *Fata Morgana*— a poem, as he commented the following summer, that "states my resistance, which is more intransigent than ever, to the masochistic enterprises in France that tend to restrict poetic freedom or to immolate it on the same altar as other freedoms."[43] As with "Full Margin"— something of a dress rehearsal for this longer work—Breton here reaches beyond the surrounding realities of the war, that "play without intermissions," toward a universe governed by wondrous marvels. The many passing references to his actual circumstances wash up like flotsam on the shore of a dream: his recollections of Mexico, memories of absent friends, the daily concerns of life at Air-Bel, his spiritual withdrawal from these bleak times, and, once more, his love for Jacqueline, the "ibis mummy" through whom he rediscovers his lost unity.

Breton also visited the other Surrealists exiled in Marseille, including Ernst, Péret, René Char, the painters Masson, Wifredo Lam, Victor Brauner, Oscar Dominguez, and others, trying to downplay the war and France's defeat with activities specifically intended to countermand their importance, practicing "desertion within oneself,"[44] as he once said in reference to Vaché. "What was most incumbent upon intellectuals at that time," Breton later explained, "was not to let this defeat—which was in no way the intellectuals' doing—remain purely military, but instead to try to turn it into a debacle of the mind."[45] The makeshift group held open-air art exhibits and played Surrealist games—tried-and-true means of combating boredom or worry—including a card game subsequently called the "Marseille Tarot," complete with a redesigned deck. One later Surrealist noted that these games were mainly a safeguard against despair, "not a matter of trying to deny the gravity of the situation [but] of preserving, at any cost, sufficient freedom of mind with respect to it."[46]

The mood, needless to say, was anything but festive, and as the borders tightened, those still in France, undesirables all from Vichy's perspective, anxiously awaited the clearances and documents that would get them out. The Bretons, among the lucky ones, were finally able to book passage in March 1941; after a stopover in Martinique (where they were at first interned, and where Breton met the poet Aimé Césaire), their ship put in to New York harbor at the beginning of June.

Even in the relative safety of New York, Breton remained preoccupied by the war, as both a threat to civilization and, more personally, an obstacle keeping him from his beloved Paris. He spent the years 1941 to 1946 in the United States, eking out a meager existence as an announcer on Voice of America radio and trying as best he could to maintain some form of cohesive group activity with his fellow expatriates, among them Duchamp, Masson, Tanguy, Ernst, Leonora Carrington, Kurt Seligmann, and the Chilean painter Matta. Few Americans were invited to these meetings, or were particularly interested. As for the uprooted Europeans, while they welcomed this Surrealist colonization of the New World, they found Breton's required café meetings and transplanted rules of order somewhat out of place in the sprawling chaos of Manhattan.

Breton's poems in this time of exile seem, more than anything, attempts to make sense of a situation that was no doubt more bewildering and frightening than the war he'd experienced on the field. One piece, simply called "War," tries to come to grips with the conflict itself, here personified as an onanistic beast, in echo perhaps (as the dedication would suggest) of Max Ernst's 1935 painting *The Angel of the*

Hearth, or perhaps of the wreckage of a cargo ship that Breton had seen during his brief military service two years earlier, "the portrait of the goddess of this war, with its great and horrible insect body and its head of armor lost in the clouds: it's both majestic and repulsive."[47] In an approach that seems typical of these years, another long poem, "The States-General," interweaves reflections, readings, daydreams, glimpses of his New York life, and a host of historical, esoteric, and political references, all suspended around a phrase that had occurred to him in half-sleep: "There will always be a wind-borne shovel in the sand of dreams." And in the book-length *Ode to Charles Fourier* (*Ode à Charles Fourier*), he combines an imaginary dialogue with the nineteenth-century utopian philosopher (*"Poverty swindling oppression slaughter* are still the same ills for which you branded civilization / Fourier they've scoffed but one day they'll have to try your remedy whether they like it or not") with postcard glimpses of his travels of the moment:

> Fourier I salute you from the Grand Canyon of Colorado
> I see the eagle soaring from your head [...]
> I salute you from the Nevada of the gold-prospector
> From the land promised and kept
> To the land rich in higher promises which it must yet keep
> From the depths of the blue ore mine which reflects the loveliest sky
> For always beyond that bar sign which continues to haunt the street
>   of a ghost town—
> Virginia-City—"The Old Blood Bucket" [...][48]

Ode to Charles Fourier was written in the summer of 1945, during a trip through the Indian villages of the American Southwest with a young woman named Elisa Claro (*née* Bindhoff). It was, in fact, a kind of honeymoon voyage, for Jacqueline, little more than a year after the Bretons' arrival in New York, had left her husband for the

American sculptor David Hare, taking Aube with her and plunging Breton into "awful, terrible depression."[49] As he described it in his book *Arcanum 17* (*Arcane 17*), "All that I had taken for indestructible in the realm of feeling had been swept away without my even knowing what gust did it: the only sign left was a child ... All the world's injustice and severity separated me from this child."[50] At the end of 1943, eighteen months after his separation from Jacqueline, Breton had met Elisa Claro in a midtown restaurant. Having recently lost her own daughter in a drowning accident, Elisa saw Breton as a salvation as much as he did her, and in 1945 the regeneration they offered each other became a marriage that would last the rest of his life.

Fourier and Breton's other American poems were published in his next collection, a self-selected anthology with the spare title *Poèmes,* which was issued in 1948. At nearly three hundred pages, the volume also contained copious selections from *Pawnshop, Earthlight, The Magnetic Fields, Soluble Fish,* and *The White-Haired Revolver,* the entirety of *The Air of Water* and *Fata Morgana,* down through works written since his repatriation to France two years earlier. Given the stocktaking and reconstruction going on throughout Europe, there is something particularly apposite about this retrospective anthology.

More specifically, the rearward glance of *Poèmes* reflected Breton's own postwar situation. Once back in France, he immediately set about trying to regroup and reignite the Surrealist movement he had left behind, much as he had tried to do in New York. But unlike the capital he remembered, Paris in the late 1940s was a city wrestling with the specters of defeat and retribution. Many of Breton's former allies, including Aragon, Eluard, Tzara, and René Char, had become prominent figures in the Stalinist PCF, which now more than ever wanted no part of independent operators like him. No doubt Char was only half joking when he wondered whether Breton ought to be shot—a less extravagant whim in those years of political purges and score-settling than it might now appear. Others, such as Tanguy, Ernst, Matta, Man Ray, Péret, and Duchamp, had remained overseas. Still others, notably Desnos and Artaud, were dead or declared clinically insane, while survivors such as Prévert, Queneau, Leiris, Masson, and Soupault were forging their own, very different lives in the aftermath of the war, and were too preoccupied or too bitter simply to pick up where their onetime comrade had left off. Nor did the public at large show much interest: when Breton organized a huge retrospective exhibition of Surrealism in 1947, seconded by a few remaining faithful and the first recruits to Surrealism's postwar roster, art critics and visitors alike tended to dismiss it as "a rehash of old tricks, worn out from overuse."[51]

For all intents and purposes, *Poèmes* was Breton's final poetic word. The war had taken its toll on this level as well, for the later poems in the collection occasionally sound an unfamiliar note of fatigue. Even the recent cycle *Xénophiles,* seven short pieces based on such far-off locales as Chile (Elisa's native land) and the South Sea islands, manages to convey little of the excitement of discovery that one would expect, or that Breton might well have felt even a decade earlier. As the poems become more conscious, more directed, and more far-flung geographically, they lose some of the adventurousness from the prewar years. Instead, Breton's true sense of exoticism emerges on home ground; his earlier writings evoke a Paris in brilliant electrical darkness, proliferating in fantastic human and animal creatures, in buildings and monuments that are the stuff of dreamscapes. The poems from *The Magnetic Fields, Earthlight,* and even *The White-Haired Revolver* create a fabulous world, at once thrillingly modern and enchantingly old-fashioned, dusty and brilliant, where the shine of "black wax" calls forth the glamorous Bakelite of 1930s telephones, and a billboard advertisement for Mazda light bulbs becomes a secular icon. Few poets have Breton's talent to turn familiar surroundings into a veritable Wonderland for adults. But the magic bleaches slowly during the years of Breton's political disillusionment and first sentimental failures, then through the period of foreign exile and anxiety and further divorce. By the time he arrives at the distant shores of *Xénophiles,* the exotic has little exoticism left in it. Instead, as one critic has written, the "exactness of the ethnological data" in the texts suggests less a cycle of verse than a "scholarly dissertation."[52] To my mind, there is more mystery in another poem of that year, whose inspiration is the most intimate of all: "On the Road to San Romano" (its title derived from Paolo Ucello's *The Battle of San Romano,* a painting Breton had long admired), the last piece in *Poèmes,* and a more fitting coda to his long and intrepid poetic journey than a decade's worth of work before it:

> Poetry is made in bed like love
> Its unmade sheets are the dawn of things [...]
> The embrace of poetry like the embrace of the naked body
> Protects while it lasts
> Against all access by the misery of the world

What was left to say? Poetically speaking, apparently very little. As the century entered its second half, France was still recovering from the war and its memories of German occupation, while the entire world cringed under the novel threat of atomic annihilation. Still politically active, Breton over the next two decades endorsed the Citizens of the World initiative, joined Camus and Sartre in the anti-Stalinist Revolutionary Democratic Rally, supported the autonomy of Celtic culture, and protested France's military involvement in Algeria. A tireless promoter of the Surrealist movement, now rebuilt with members who were not yet born when the first *Manifesto* was conceived, he coauthored numerous tracts on a variety of issues, and in 1952 he published a series of radio interviews that gave a mainstream audience its first comprehensive overview of Surrealism's history and aspirations. But for many, Breton's days as a significant intellectual presence were largely over, and as time went on he, and Surrealism, would increasingly be relegated to the past by a generation successively distracted by Existentialism, the New Novel, and Pop Art—notwithstanding his fervent protests to the contrary. Only after his death on 28 September 1966, at the age of seventy, would the lasting impact of Surrealism begin to be recognized, as students adopted his phrases during the May 1968 riots and the disquieting aesthetic of Surrealist art infiltrated the visual idiom of everyday life. But for now, very little verse, automatic or otherwise, flowed from his pen.

When Breton did complete another book of poems, in 1959, his inspiration was still more distant and exotic than the faraway climes of *Xénophiles*—to the constellations themselves, as depicted in twenty-two gouaches by the former Surrealist painter Joan Miró. The short prose poems, written as an accompaniment to works Miró had executed nearly two decades before, were Breton's lyrical response to the painter's "*floodgates* from which spurt, at one bound, love and liberty."[53]

And yet, ultimately, the "mouth of shadows" proved not to be entirely silenced. Two years after *Constellations,* and five before his death, Breton published what might be considered his last volume of poems, slight though it may be: *Le La* (an expression that suggests "setting the tone"), a mere four sentences obtained during the 1950s, as *The Magnetic Fields* had been over thirty years earlier, by listening to the fleeting, insistent, enigmatic phrases that occasionally "knocked

Breton in the 1950s, at his house in Saint-Cirq-Lapopie. *Courtesy Sylvie Sator.*

at the window." The message comes full circle; the seeker rounds the world and returns home.

Breton set out the value of such phrases in a brief preliminary text, in terms that could apply to the poetic achievement of a lifetime:

> The (active-passive) experience of listening to the "dictation of thought" (or of something else?), to which Surrealism originally wished to subject itself and subscribe through so-called "automatic" writing, is, as I have already stated, exposed to many random occurrences in waking life. Those sentences or fragments of sentences, therefore, have immediately been valuable: scraps of monologue or dialogue extracted from sleep and retained without any possibility of error, so distinct do their articulation and intonation remain at awakening ... However sibylline they might be, on every possible occasion I have collected them with the careful consideration owed to precious stones ... Even if, by a wide margin, the "mouth of shadows" did not speak to me with the same generosity as it did to Hugo and was even content to make desultory remarks, what matters is that it was willing to suggest some words that for me remain a *touchstone* ... As discouraging as they may be as far as a literal interpretation is concerned, on an emotional level these words were made to set the *tone* for me.[54]

"On an emotional level": in the final account, this phrase summarizes as well as any the lasting and insinuating seduction of Breton's poetry. Trying to quantify seduction is a fruitless exercise; Breton himself, who "loathed the cerebral,"[55] once remarked that he counted himself "among the disciples of the man who said, 'Criticism will be love, or will not be at all.'"[56] No doubt the purest expression of that seduction lies in the variegated influence Breton's poems have had, first on the poets who surrounded him—Eluard, Desnos, Benjamin Péret, so many others—then, either directly or through these latter, on several generations of poets in their wake. A haphazard list, to take only the British and Americans, would have to include David Gascoyne,

Charles Henri Ford, Frank O'Hara, John Ashbery, Ron Padgett, Kenneth Koch (the entire New York School would be hard to imagine without Breton), Andrei Codrescu, Philip Lamantia, the Beats, Clayton Eshleman, Jerome Rothenberg, and, to some degree, Charles Olson, W. S. Merwin, Diane Wakowski, and Robert Kelly—not to mention the poets whose translations are included in this book, and who have melded the affinities between Breton's poems and their own in these recastings of his verse. One of these poets, Bill Zavatsky, surely speaks for many of his colleagues when he hazards that a "great glory" of this poetry is "the gorgeous, often wild, often unexpected images that animate it. We have no idea where the most powerful of them are coming from, or where they are going (except deep into our own hearts and minds), and what they are going to couple with to create metaphors—connections—as compelling as any poet has ever made."[57]

For myself, I can well remember my first encounters with automatic writing in adolescence, at a time when I was already practicing a similar kind of writing without yet knowing that others (many others) had gone before me. The discovery of such meanderings in *The Magnetic Fields* and *Soluble Fish* impressed me as exciting, encouraging, and inexplicably *right*. Later, the heady bravado of the manifestoes chipped away at the stultifying shackles of academic discourse, while the wild, spectacular adventures of the Surrealist group seemed a heroic burst of living color in a mournful and monochromatic world. And then there was the poetry itself, especially the early poems, not necessarily the best but so daredevil in their exploration of things normally kept outside the poetic preserve, their encyclopedic appropriation of so many disparate elements, the self-contained, self-generated *adventure* that played out in their lines. That a world so far outside could emanate from one so far inside, that the placement of letters on a page could open such secret doors—this was true earthly magic, sweeping everything away and reassembling it, and then reassembling it again, and again. The youthful poems I derived from "Sunflower," "Black Forest," and others are a long-forgotten embarrassment. But as Rimbaud reminds us, how wholesome is the wind! No matter which way this wind blows, the important thing is that, eight decades later, it is still howling through the lines that follow.

Any anthology editor will tell you that the pleasures of assembly are more than counterbalanced by the sorrows of omission, and the present case is no different. Specifically, I have left out the book-length poem *Ode to Charles Fourier,* judging that a mere slice will never give the flavor of the whole, and I have been able to give only woefully short excerpts of longer works such as *Soluble Fish* and *Fata Morgana.* I have also omitted the cycle *Constellations,* recently published in English, because of both its availability and its codependence on Miró's paintings. That said, I have endeavored to represent every major phase of Breton's development, so that the following pages might be read as a concise autobiography of his poetic evolution. I also confess to having left room for some strictly personal preferences, poems that have appealed to me in some indefinable way since I first discovered his work, without their necessarily being crucial to the opus.

Most of all, I have tried to highlight the elements that set Breton's poems apart from those of his contemporaries: the curious fusion of antiquated sensibility and modernist expression; the marriage of the coolly cerebral and the ardently romantic; the immediacy and accessibility, even when hermetically draped, that made a poem such as "Plutôt la vie" ("Choose Life"), already half a century old at the time, an attractive banner for student rebellion in 1968; and the luminous traces of a life lived both in the glare of public action and in the deep shadows of himself.

Mark Polizzotti, August 2002

NOTES

1 Breton to Théodore Fraenkel, 22 June 1914, in Marguerite Bonnet, *André Breton, naissance de l'aventure surréaliste* (Paris: José Corti, 1975), 32.

2 "Arthur Rimbaud," in AB, *Anthology of Black Humor,* trans. Mark Polizzotti (San Francisco: City Lights Books, 1997), 164.

3 This and the previous quote are from "Clearly," in AB, *The Lost Steps,* trans. Mark Polizzotti (Lincoln: University of Nebraska Press, 1996), 81.

4 "Reply to a Survey," in *The Lost Steps,* 83.

5 *Manifesto of Surrealism,* in AB, *Manifestoes of Surrealism,* trans. Richard Seaver and Helen R. Lane (Ann Arbor: University of Michigan Press, 1969), 40.

6 "The Disdainful Confession," in *The Lost Steps,* 6.

7 "Portrait étrange" (unpublished poem, 1913), in AB, *Oeuvres complètes,* I, ed. Marguerite Bonnet et al. (Paris: Gallimard ["Bibliothèque de la Pléiade"], 1988), 32.

8 "Le Rêve," in ibid., 29. Dated September 1911, the poem was first published—or, at least, printed—in Breton's high school literary magazine, *Vers l'Idéal,* under the pseudonym "René Dobrant."

9 AB, *Conversations: The Autobiography of Surrealism,* trans. Mark Polizzotti (New York: Paragon House, 1993), 4.

10 Ibid., 9.

11 Ibid., 13.

12 AB to Guillaume Apollinaire, 15 August 1916, in Bonnet, *André Breton,* 52.

13 Ibid.

14 Jacques Vaché to AB, 29 April 1917; for Vaché's rank, see Vaché to his mother, 30 June 1915. This and Vaché's other letters are quoted from Jacques Vaché, *Soixante-dix-neuf lettres de guerre,* ed. Georges Sebbag (Paris: Jean-Michel Place, 1989).

15 Jacques Vaché to Théodore Fraenkel, 16 June 1917.

16 "As in a Wood," in AB, *Free Rein,* trans. Michel Parmentier and Jacqueline d'Amboise (Lincoln: University of Nebraska Press, 1995), 236.

17 "Disdainful Confession," 2.

18 *Manifesto,* 19–20.

19 AB to Théodore Fraenkel, 21 October 1917, in *Oeuvres complètes,* I, 1231.

20 Jacques Vaché to AB, 9 May 1918.

21 AB to Jacques Doucet, 4 January 1921. Unless otherwise noted, quotes from Breton's unpublished correspondence are extracted from Mark Polizzotti, *Revolution of the Mind: The Life of André Breton* (New York: Farrar, Straus and Giroux, 1995).

22 AB to Tristan Tzara, 20 April 1919, in Michel Sanouillet, *Dada à Paris* (Paris: Jean-Jacques Pauvert, 1965), 444.

23 Aragon, "Dada" (unpublished ms., December 1922), in Roger Garaudy, *L'Itinéraire d'Aragon: du surréalisme au monde réel* (Paris: Gallimard, 1961), 82.

24 "Lecture on Dada" (September 1922), in Tristan Tzara, *Seven Dada Manifestos and Lampisteries,* trans. Barbara Wright (London: John Calder, 1977), 112.

25 *Manifesto,* 21–23.

26 All quotes from Maurice Nadeau, *The History of Surrealism,* trans. Richard Howard (Cambridge, Mass.: Harvard University Press, 1989), 86.

27 *Conversations,* 50.

28 *Comoedia* (7 February 1922). Another friend who fell by the wayside at around this time was the painter Francis Picabia, who had supported Breton in his spat with Tzara, but who angrily broke off relations when Breton launched the Surrealist movement.

29 *Manifesto,* 47.

30 Ibid., 36.

31 Ibid., 26.

32 Ibid., 14.

33 Ibid., 9.

34 AB, "Tu es grave ..." (unpublished poem, ca. end 1924), in *Oeuvres complètes,* I, 609–10.

35 AB to Lise Meyer, 26 February 1925, in AB, *Oeuvres complètes,* II, ed. Marguerite Bonnet et al. (Paris: Gallimard ["Bibliothèque de la Pléiade"], 1992), 1442n.

36 André Thirion, *Revolutionaries without a Revolution,* trans. Joachim Neugroschel (New York: Macmillan, 1975), 125.

37 AB to Simone Breton, 25 November 1927.

38 *Second Manifesto of Surrealism,* in AB, *Manifestoes,* 131.

39 "The Automatic Message," in AB, *Break of Day,* trans. Mark Polizzotti and Mary Ann Caws (Lincoln: University of Nebraska Press, 1999), 130, 139.

40 "Lightning Rod," in *Anthology of Black Humor,* xix, xvi.

41 AB to Jean Paulhan, 25 November 1939.

42 *Conversations,* 154.

43 Ibid., 188.

44 "Jacques Vaché," in *Anthology of Black Humor,* 293.

45 *Conversations,* 154.

46 Jean-Louis Bédouin, *Vingt ans de surréalisme, 1939–1959* (Paris: Denoel, 1961), 27.

47 AB to Jacqueline Breton, 5 April 1940, in AB, *Oeuvres complètes,* III, ed. Etienne-Alain Hubert et al. (Paris: Gallimard ["Bibliothèque de la Pléïade"], 1999), 1146–47.

48 AB, *Ode to Charles Fourier* (1945), trans. Kenneth White (New York: Grossman, 1970), n.p.

49 AB to Benjamin Péret, 27 August 1942.

50 AB, *Arcanum 17,* trans. Zack Rogow (Los Angeles: Sun & Moon Press, 1994), 69.

51 *Les Lettres françaises* (18 July 1947), in José Pierre, ed., *Tracts surréalistes et déclarations collectives,* II (1940–1969) (Paris: Eric Losfeld/Le Terrain Vague, 1982), 190.

52 Jean-Claude Blachère, *Les Totems d'André Breton: Surréalisme et primitivisme littéraire* (Paris: L'Harmattan, 1996), 240.

53 AB, "Constellations of Joan Miró," in Paul Hammond, *Constellations of Miró, Breton* [includes a full translation of Breton's *Constellations*] (San Francisco: City Lights Books, 2000), 194.

54 AB, preface to *Le La* (December 1960), in Jean-Pierre Cauvin and Mary Ann Caws, ed. and trans., *Poems of André Breton: A Bilingual Anthology* (Austin: University of Texas Press, 1982), 229 (trans. slightly revised).

55 Charles Duits, *André Breton a-t-il dit passe* (Paris: Denoël ["Dossiers des Lettres Nouvelles"], 1969), 78.

56 AB to Simone Kahn [Breton], 1 September 1920.

57 Bill Zavatsky, introduction to AB, *Earthlight,* trans. Bill Zavatsky and Zack Rogow (Los Angeles: Sun & Moon Press, 1993), 15.

KEY TO TRANSLATORS

D A *David Antin*

P A *Paul Auster*

S B *Samuel Beckett*

M B *Michael Benedikt*

J P C *Jean-Pierre Cauvin*

M A C *Mary Ann Caws*

R D *Robert Duncan*

D G *David Gascoyne*

H R L *Helen R. Lane*

M P *Mark Polizzotti*

E R *Edouard Roditi*

Z R *Zack Rogow*

R S *Richard Seaver*

C S *Charles Simic*

R T *Richard Tillinghast*

K W *Keith Waldrop*

B Z *Bill Zavatsky*

POEMS

MERRY

for Paul Valéry

Merry, and perhaps so imprudently laureled
With youth that a hastening fawn would enlace
This Nymph on the rocks who the soul (If not depict
Did I at least catch her in the blue of some forest edge).

On the gilded barque of a ventured dream
—Who sparked your hope? Your faith in life?—
Beyond eyes the steady rise would gleam
Under cool azure, in the whispered light . . .

—Rather than the Eden to which her hand invites,
She, ecstatic, undressed in white,
Whom reality has not yet enchained:

Caress of dawn, a statue's awe foretokened,
Awakening, avowal that one daren't, and modesty ill-feigned,
Chaste candor of a single prayer unspoken.

1913 • MP

WAY

Fondness strews you with brocaded
taffeta plans,
except where the sheen of gold found its delight.
Let July, mad
witness, at least count the sin
of the old novel for little girls that we read!

With little girls we
courted
dampens (Years, window blinds on the brink of oblivion), failing
to nurse at the sweet torrent,
—Further pleasure what chosen deed initiates you?—
a future, a dazzling Batavian Court.

Labelling
balm vain love, have we guaranteed
by our coldness
a foundation, more than hours but, months? The girls

are making batiste: Forever!—Anyway the smell annihilates
this jealous spring,

Dear young ladies.

1916 • BZ & ZR

AGE

Dawn, farewell! I'm coming out of the haunted forest; I'm braving the roads, torrid crosses. A foliage that gives blessings is ruining me. August, like a millstone, has no cracks.

Keep the panoramic view, inhale space, and mechanically unwind coils of smoke.

I'm going to choose myself a precarious enclosure: if we need to, we'll step over the boxwood. The province with heated begonias chatters, tidies up. How nicely griffons band together on the wavy flounces of skirts!

Where to look for it, since the fountains? I'm wrong to trust its bubble necklace....

Eyes in front of the sweet peas.

•

Congealed shirts on the chair. A silk hat with reflections. Man.... A mirror avenges you and treats me, the conquered one, like a stripped-off uniform. The moment returns to paw my flesh.

Houses, I'm breaking free of parched walls. We're shaking it off! A tender bed is teased about crowns.

Achieve the overwhelming poetry of staircase landings.

19 FEBRUARY 1916* · BZ & ZR

---

*Although dated 19 February (his twentieth birthday) by Breton,
the poem "Age" was actually composed on the 10th.*

BLACK FOREST*

Out

Tender capsule   etc. derby
Madame de Saint-Gobain finds time goes by slowly when alone
A cutlet wilts

                              Outline of fate
Where   shutterless   this white gable
        Waterfalls
                    Log-haulers are favored

                                        It's blowing
What a wholesome wind   the wind from the dairies

                        The author of The Guardian Angel Inn
Died last year anyhow
By the way

From Tübingen to meet me
Come young Kepler Hegel
And the faithful friend

RIMBAUD SPEAKING.

1 APRIL 1918 · BZ & ZR

FOR LAFCADIO

The avenue   meanwhile   the Gulf Stream
MAMvivary
My Mistress
takes her pet
name well Our friends
are at ease
    We get along

    Clerk
speak MAMAternal tongue
    What a bore, all that talk about "dear body"
drear body
    I'll never win all these wars

Soldier
what does my verse matter the slow drive
low drive
Better to have it said
that André Breton
collector of Indirect Loans
is dabbling in collage
while waiting to retire

1918 · MP

MISTER V

for Paul Valéry

                       In place of l'étoile
The Arc de Triomphe
which only looks like a magnet because of its amorous shape
                       shall I silver
                       the hanging gardens

LULLABY
The child with the ribbon bonnet
The child that the sea tickles.

Growing up
he looks at himself in a pearly shell
            the iris of his eye is the star
I was talking about

MARCH
Peter or Paul

He gets ready to play find the king
        today as elsewhere
his equals
    Dreams of revolutions

        It's impossible for art to depict
        The device that can catch the blue fox

         1918 · BZ & ZR

The Mystery Corset

My lovely readers,

from having to see **stars before your eyes**
Splendid maps, *with lighting effects,* Venice

Back then the furniture in my room was solidly anchored to the
walls and I had myself strapped in it to write:
I've found my sea legs

we belong to a kind of sentimental **Touring Club**

A CASTLE IN PLACE OF A HEAD
it's also the **Charity Bazaar**

Games are fun for all ages;
                    Poetic games, etc.
I hold Paris like—if I may show you the future—your open hand

a tightly bound waist.

1919 • MP

from THE MAGNETIC FIELDS

HONEYMOON

To what are mutual attractions due? There are some jealousies more touching than others. I willingly wander in such baffling darkness as that of the rivalry between a woman and a book. The finger on the side of the forehead is not the barrel of a revolver. I believe that although we paid heed to each other's thinking, the automatic "Of nothing" that is our proudest denial did not once need to be uttered during the whole wedding spree. Lower than the stars there is nothing to stare at. No matter what train you may be travelling in, it is dangerous to lean out of the carriage-door window. The stations were plainly distributed about a bay. The sea that to the human eye is never so beautiful as the sky did not leave us. In the depths of our eyes disappeared neat reckonings bearing on the future like those of prison walls.   ∎

Getting bored cannot be done; that would be to the detriment of caresses and before long we shall be there no more.

The great legend of the railways and reservoirs, the weariness of carriage animals, easily affect the hearts of certain men. Here are some who have had experience of driving-belts: regular breathing has become a thing of the past for them. I can say without fear of contradiction that industrial accidents are more seemly than prudent marriages. It can however happen that the boss's daughter crosses the courtyard. It is easier to get rid of a grease-stain than a dead leaf; at least one's hand does not tremble. Equidistant from the workshops for manufacture and those for decoration the prism of supervision plays maliciously with the star of enlistment.

·

What are we waiting for? A woman? Two trees? Three flags? What are we waiting for? Nothing.

·

The pointer pigeons that cause travellers to be murdered bear a blue-edged letter in their beaks.

·

Between the manifold splendours of anger, I watch a door slam like the corsage of a flower or the india-rubber used by schoolchildren.

·

The scavengers of paradise are well acquainted with those white rats that run up and down beneath God's throne.

·

I was born on All Souls'-day in a frightful meadow amongst shells and stag-beetles.

■

Sun of the astral seas, torpedoing of the black beams of great long-boats, uneasiness corridor and glares of capers, of muscatels, of mara-schinos! Darling, where is that acrobat, where the little nest in which I was born? My friend's horse is a bisected thoroughbred, it runs across country and emits flames from its dusty nostrils. Its gallop is stronger than the night, more powerful than the ethereal emanations of love. When shall we be able to grasp between our thighs this mammiferous monster, this Tibetan goat which clambers on the Gaurisankar to the sound of metal flutes sweeter than your cry, O desolate shepherd? We shall see blood-tinged blotting-pads and pastel blue faces. They will be greenly adorned by light and by plaited leaves. Their eyes are of a pale grey shade that makes men tremble and women have miscarriages.

■

Temptation to order a new refreshment: a plantaneous demolition, for instance.

■

Present from the earliest hour, the white herring polishes the counter and that creates a reek of poetry, which famishes.

■

Today or some other day they'll forget to light the street-lamps.

■

Do not disturb the genius who plants white roots, my subterranean nerve-endings.

WITH PHILIPPE SOUPAULT; JUNE 1919 • DG

COUNTERFEIT COIN

to Benjamin Péret

From the vase of crystal made in Bohemia
From the vase of cry
From the vase of cry
From the vase of
Of crystal
From the vase of crystal made in Bohemia
Bohemia
Bohemia
Of crystal made in Bohemia
Bohemia
Bohemia
Bohemia
Hem hem yes Bohemia
From the vase of crystal made in Bo Bo
From the vase of crystal made in Bohemia
To the bubbles you blew as a child
You blew
You blew

Ew

Ew

You blew

You blew as a child

From the vase of crystal made in Bohemia

To the bubbles you blew as a child

You blew

You blew

Yes you blew as a child

That's it that's it the whole poem

Emeral dawn

Emeral dawn

Reflections' ephemeral dawn

Emeral dawn

Emeral dawn

Reflections' ephemeral dawn

MARCH 1920 · BZ & ZR

Neuilly 1-18	Breton, model dairy, 12 R. de l'Ouest, Neuilly.
Nord 13-40	Breton (E.) fun. monum., 23 Av. Cimetière Parisien, Pantin.
Passy 44-15	Breton (Eug.), wines, rest., cigars, 176 R. de la Pompe.
Roquette 07-90	Breton (François), veterinarian, 21 R. Trousseau, (11th).
Central 64-99	Breton Bros., engineers, 262 R. de Belleville, (20th).
Bergère 43-61	Breton and Son, 12 R. Rougement, (9th).
Archives 32-58	Breton (G.), automotive, cycle suppl., 78 R. des Archives, (3rd).
Central 30-08	Breton (Georges), 4 R. du Marché-Saint-Honoré, (1st).
Wagram 60-84	Breton (Mr. and Mrs. G.), 58 Blvd. Malesherbes, (8th).
Gutenburg 03-78	Breton (H.), laces, 60 R. de Richelieu, (2nd).
Passy 80-70	Breton (Henri), wholesaler, 22 R. Octave-Feuillet, (16th).
Gobelins 08-09	Breton (J.), Combier Elix., main off., 21-23 Butte du Rhône.

Roquette 32-59	Breton (J.-L.), representative, undr.-secr. State, inviol., 81½ Blvd. Soult.
Archives 39-43	Breton (L.), hotel-bar, 38 R. François-Miron, (4th).
Marcadet 04-11	Breton (Noel), hotel-rest., 56 Blvd. National, Clichy.
Roquette 02-25	Breton (Paul), lathe operator, 21 R. Saint-Maur, (11th).
Central 84-08	Breton (Th.), law office, 13 R. du Fg. Montmartre, (9th).
Saxe 57-86	Breton (J.), cookies, 16-18 R. La Quintinie, (15th).
Archives 35-44	Breton (J.) and Co., wholesale paper, 245 R. Saint-Martin, (3rd).
Roquette 09-76	Breton and Co., Inc., wholesale coal, 60 Q. La Rapée, (12th).

Breton (André)

1920 · BZ & ZR

NO WAY OUT OF HERE

for Paul Eluard

Freedom the color of man
What mouths will fly apart
Tiles
Under the thrust of that monstrous vegetation

The sun a sleeping dog
Abandons the steps of a rich villa

Languid blue breast where beats the heart of time

A naked girl in the arms of a dancer handsome and armor-plated
    like Saint George
But that's for much later
Feeble Atlantes

                    ■

River of stars
Who carry off the punctuation marks in my poem and those of
    my friends

We mustn't forget that the lot I drew gave me this freedom and you
If it's she I conquered
Who else but you arrives sliding down a strand of frost
That explorer grappling with the fire ants of his own blood
It's the same month of the year right to the end
Perspective that allows us to judge whether we're dealing with souls
     or not
19 .. A lieutenant in the artillery awaits in a trail of gunpowder

                                             ■

Just as well the first-come
Bent over the oval of internal desire
Numbers these bushes by dint of glowworms
Depending on whether you'll stretch out your hand for a headstand
     or before making love

As everyone knows

In the other world that will not exist
I see you white and elegant
Women's hair gives off a scent of acanthus leaves
O superimposed panes of thought
In the glass earth rattle glass skeletons

                                             ■

Everyone has heard of the Raft of the Medusa
And if need be can imagine such a raft in the sky

20 MAY 1923 · MP

IN THE EYES OF THE GODS

to Louis Aragon

"A little before midnight down by the docks.
If a disheveled woman follows you don't pay any attention.
It's the azure. You don't have to be afraid of the azure.
There'll be a large blond vase in a tree.
The bell tower of the town with blended colors
Will be your reference point. Take your time,
Remember. The brown geyser hurling fern shoots into the sky
Salutes you."
            The letter sealed with a fish's three corners
Was now passing by in the light of the suburbs
Like an animal tamer's sign.
                  All the same,
The beautiful woman, the victim, the one known
In the neighborhood as the little reseda pyramid
Unstitched just for herself a cloud like
A sachet of pity.
             Later the white armor
Which used to take care of household and other chores

Taking it easy now more than ever,
The child with the seashell, the one supposed to be ...
But shh.
                        A brazier was already baring
Its breast to a delightful cloak-
And-dagger story.
                                On the bridge, at the same time,
Like so the cat-headed dew rocked back and forth.
Night,—and their illusions would be lost.

Here are the white Fathers coming back from vespers
With the immense key hanging above them.
Here are the gray heralds; finally here's her letter
Or her lip: my heart is a cuckoo for God.

But by the time she speaks, nothing's left except a wall
Flapping inside a tomb like an unbleached sail.
Eternity searches for a wristwatch
A little before midnight down by the docks.

                14 JULY 1923 · BZ & ZR

CHOOSE LIFE

Choose life instead of those prisms with no depth even if their colors
    are purer
Instead of this hour always hidden instead of these terrible vehicles
    of cold flame
Instead of these overripe stones
Choose this heart with its safety catch
Instead of that murmuring pool
And that white fabric singing in the air and the earth at the same time
Instead of that marriage blessing joining my forehead to total vanity's
                 Choose life

Choose life with its conspiratorial sheets
Its scars from escapes
Choose life choose that rose window on my tomb
The life of being here nothing but being here
Where one voice says Are you there where another answers Are you
    there
I'm hardly here at all alas
And even when we might be making fun of what we kill
                 Choose life

Choose life choose life venerable Childhood
The ribbon coming out of a fakir
Resembles the playground slide of the world
Though the sun is only a shipwreck
Insofar as a woman's body resembles it
You dream contemplating the whole length of its trajectory
Or only while closing your eyes on the adorable storm named your hand
Choose life

Choose life with its waiting rooms
When you know you'll never be shown in
Choose life instead of those health spas
Where you're served by drudges
Choose life unfavorable and long
When the books close again here on less gentle shelves
And when over there the weather would be better than better it would
   be free yes
Choose life

Choose life as the pit of scorn
With that head beautiful enough
Like the antidote to that perfection it summons and it fears
Life the makeup on God's face

Life like a virgin passport
A little town like Pont-à-Mousson
And since everything's already been said
Choose life instead

1923 · BZ & ZR

SUNFLOWER

for Pierre Reverdy

The traveler who crossed Les Halles at summer's end
Walked on tiptoe
Despair rolled its great handsome lilies across the sky
And in her handbag was my dream that flask of salts
That only God's godmother had breathed
Torpors unfurled like mist
At the Chien qui Fume
Where pro and con had just entered
They could hardly see the young woman and then only at an angle
Was I dealing with the ambassadress of saltpeter
Or with the white curve on black background we call thought
The Innocents' Ball was in full swing
The Chinese lanterns slowly caught fire in chestnut trees
The shadowless lady knelt on the Pont-au-Change
On Rue Gît-le-Coeur the stamps had changed
The night's promises had been kept at last
The carrier pigeons and emergency kisses
Merged with the beautiful stranger's breasts

Jutting beneath the crepe of perfect meanings
A farm prospered in the heart of Paris
And its windows looked out on the Milky Way
But no one lived there yet because of the guests
Guests who are known to be more faithful than ghosts
Some like that woman appear to be swimming
And a bit of their substance becomes part of love
She internalizes them
I am the plaything of no sensory power
And yet the cricket who sang in hair of ash
One evening near the statue of Etienne Marcel
Threw me a knowing glance
André Breton it said pass

26 AUGUST 1923 • MP

A burst of laughter
in sapphire from the Island of Ceylon

The prettiest straws
HAVE PALE FACES
UNDER LOCK AND KEY

on an isolated farm
DAY BY DAY
the pleasant
grows worse

A well-paved road
leads you to the edge of the unknown

coffee
looks out for number one
THE DAILY ARTISAN OF YOUR BEAUTY
M^ADAM,

a pair
# of silk stockings
is not

A leap into the void

A KITE

Love, first

It could all turn out so well

PARIS IS JUST A BIG TOWN

Watch out for

The fire smoldering beneath

THE PRAYER

Of fine weather

Know that

Ultra-violet rays

have completed their task

Short and sweet

THE FIRST WHITE NEWSPAPER

OF CHANCE

Red will be

The wandering minstrel

WHERE IS HE?

in memory

in his house

AT THE LOVERS' BALL

I do

as I dance

What has been done, what will be done

1924 • MP

from SOLUBLE FISH

In those days the one thing people were all talking about around the place de la Bastille was an enormous wasp that went down the boulevard Richard-Lenoir in the morning singing at the top of its lungs and asking the children riddles. The little modern sphinx had already made quite a few victims when, as I left the café whose façade some thought would look good with a cannon, although the Prison in the neighborhood may pass today for a legendary building, I met the wasp with the waist of a pretty woman and it asked me the way.

"Good heavens, my pretty one, it is not up to me to put a point on your lipstick. The sky-slate has just been wiped clean and you know that miracles no longer happen except between seasons. Go back home; you live on the fourth floor of a nice-looking building and even though your windows look out on the court, you will perhaps find some way not to bother me any more."

The insect's buzzing, as unbearable as a lung congestion, at this moment drowned out the noise of the tram-ways, whose trolley was a dragonfly. The wasp, after having looked at me for a long time, no doubt for the purpose of conveying to me its ironical surprise, now approached me and said in my ear: "I'll be back." It did disappear, as a matter of fact, and I was already delighted to be rid of it so easily when I noticed that the Genius of the place, ordinarily very alert, seemed to be having an attack of vertigo and be on the verge of falling on people passing by. This could only be a hallucination on my part, due to the great heat: the sun, moreover, kept me from concluding that there had been a sudden transmission of natural powers, for it was like a long aspen leaf, and I had only to close my eyes to hear the motes of dust sing.

The wasp, whose approach had nonetheless made me feel most uncomfortable (people for several days now had been talking about the exploits of mysterious stingers that respected neither the coolness of subways nor the solitude of the woods), had not completely ceased having her say.

Not far from there, the Seine was inexplicably carrying along an adorably polished woman's torso, although it had no head or members, and a few hooligans who had pointed it out not long before maintained that this torso was an intact body, but a new body, a body such as had never been seen before, never been caressed before. The police, who were worn out, were deeply moved, but since the boat that had been launched to pursue the new Eve had never come back, they had given up a second more costly expedition, and there had been an unconfirmed report that the beautiful palpitating white breasts had never belonged to a living creature of the sort that still haunts our desires. She was beyond our desires, like flames, and she was, as it were, the first day of the feminine season of flame, just one March 21st of snow and pearls.

1924 · RS & HRL

Make it so daylight does not yet enter
Who's there?
With his cages full of red wheels
Let him finish setting his egrets outside
A rose window of sky-colored grass on which you walk
Between the cobblestones
I see silent caravans much like an accordion on a table
I see the water flowers arranged by species along a riverbank you are
    following
I see night such as birds make with their great square eyes
Birds that have a mirror relationship with fireflies
Night does not knock at the glass door it spends its time in the closet
Amid the blue and green linens it sings it zigzags through the house
In the name of the forest and the sea
Which one is darker which one do you dare name more often
With lips that make me see the forest and ocean
One inside another when the wind scatters the great written sheets
And the grass rises in the dimming lamps
Not long ago in the country they built large iron constructions
Which are beautiful and tall and like my love
Armatures that are good only for love and the sky
They still don't know what they are used for

The geniuses that watch over your hands to keep them from lighting,
    lighting
In the beam of a lighthouse I see white ships falling into distress one
    by one
The geniuses that watch over your hands over your eyes so that they'll
    be like spinning pins
In the wheels of bird cages
And also graceful quartz quadrilaterals under the worn pickax of men
    beaten down by emotion
Go all around the world while you sleep
Thinking that time sets off like a shot
In front in front of everything you consider
Marvelous in appearance like a gyroscope on the lip of a glass
Or like the white screen whose patience is made of so much haste,
    desire, drama, and pursuit
While you are caressed by the palm of tears
And by eternal leisure that brings delight
Glad and sorrowful almost in equal measure
Like those butterflies that look too much like leaves like soldiers
    running on glaciers
I see your huge portraits
Because of a braid of hair ten times too long
I see the ice crack beneath the soldiers
Everything is silent as in the most wonderful days of the ark
The imagination is a flower bed of broken lances
In imagination I find only the heart's grace
I see the Templars in their immemorial cowl
They are scattered and distant in my dream
What I adore what nothing could ever make me burn
Thou Suzanne the very shape of fire

29 AUGUST 1928 · MP

I LISTEN TO MYSELF
STILL TALKING

Mad as I am
I am not at death's door
I tear out the shrubs arresting the suicide at cliff's edge
Animals in my traps decay where they're caught
It's practically only dusk that gets their scent
Dusk riddled with shot that my exhausted hounds can't catch

I hold in my arms women who want only to be with another
Women who in love hear wind crossing the poplars
Women who in hate are taller and slimmer than praying mantises
It's for me they invented unbuilding blocks
A thousand times more beautiful than card games

And I laid the blame on absence
In all its shapes
And I held in my arms apparitions under the mark
Of ashes and loves newer than the first
That ever closed my eyes my hope my jealousy

WITH PAUL ELUARD AND RENÉ CHAR; MARCH 1930 • KW

THE WRITINGS DEPART

The satin of pages we turn in books bodies forth a woman so beautiful
That when we aren't reading we contemplate this woman sadly
Without daring to speak to her without daring to tell her that she's
    so beautiful
That what we're going to find out is priceless
This woman passes imperceptibly in a rustling of flowers
Sometimes she turns around in the printed seasons
And asks the time or even pretends to look jewels straight in the eye
The way real creatures don't
And the world dies a break appears in the rings of the air
A rip in the surface of the heart
The morning papers bring women singers whose voices are the color
    of sand on soft dangerous shores
And sometimes the afternoon papers make way for very young girls
    who lead animals on chains
But most beautiful of all is the space between certain letters
Where hands whiter than dog-eared stars at noon
Ravage a nest of white swallows
To make it rain forever
So low so low that their wings can't mingle with it any more

Hands which lead us to arms so delicate that the meadow mist in its
    graceful interlacing above the pools is their imperfect mirror
Arms joined to none other than the amazing danger of a body made
    for love
Whose belly summons detached sighs of bushes full of veils
And which has nothing earthly about it but the immense icy truth of
    the sleighs of glances on the totally white expanse
Of what I'll never see again
Because of a marvelous bandage
My own in the blindman's buff of wounds

CA. 1930 • BZ & ZR

THE FOREST IN THE AXE

Someone just died but I'm still alive and yet I don't have a soul any more. All I have left is a transparent body inside of which transparent doves hurl themselves on a transparent dagger held by a transparent hand. I see struggle in all its beauty, real struggle which nothing can measure, just before the last star comes out. The rented body I live in like a hut detests the soul I had which floats in the distance. It's time to put an end to that famous dualism for which I've been so much re-proached. Gone are the days when eyes without light and rings drew sediment from the pools of color. There's neither red nor blue any more. Unanimous red-blue fades away in turn like a robin redbreast in the hedges of inattention. Someone just died,—not you or I or they exactly, but all of us, except me who survives by a variety of means: I'm still cold for example. That's enough. A match! A match! Or how about some rocks so I can split them, or some birds so I can follow them, or some corsets so I can tighten them around dead women's waists, so they'll come back to life and love me, with their exhausting hair, their disheveled glances! A match, so no one dies for brandied plums, a match so the Italian straw hat can be more than a play! Hey, lawn! Hey, rain! *I'm* the unreal breath of this garden. The black crown resting on my head is a cry of migrating crows because up till now there have only been those who were buried alive, and only a few of them, and here I am the first *aerated dead man*. But I have a body so I can stop doing myself in, so I can force reptiles to admire me. Bloody hands, mistletoe eyes, a mouth of dried leaves and glass (the dried leaves move under the glass; they're not as red as one would think, when indifference exposes its voracious methods), hands to gather you, miniscule thyme of my dreams, rosemary of my extreme pallor. I don't have a shadow anymore, either. Ah my shadow, my dear shadow. I should write a long letter to the shadow I lost. I'd begin it My Dear Shadow. Shadow, my darling. You see. There's no more sun. There's only one tropic left out of two. There's only one man left in a thousand. There's only one woman left in the absence of thought that characterizes in pure black this cursed era. That woman holds a bouquet of everlastings shaped like my blood.

CA. 1931 · BZ & ZR

NO GROUNDS FOR PROSECUTION

Art of days art of nights
The scale of wounds called Pardon
Red scale that quivers under the weight of a wing
When the snow-necked horsemen with empty hands
Push their vaporous chariots across the meadows
I see this scale jumping madly up and down
I see the graceful ibis
Returning from the pool laced within my heart
The wheels of the charming dream and its splendid ruts
Mounting high upon the shells of their dresses
And surprise bounding wildly over the sea
Depart my darling dawn forget nothing of my life
Take these roses creeping in the mirror-well
Take every beating of every lid
Take everything down to the threads that hold the steps of rope and
    waterdrop dancers
Art of days art of nights
I stand before a distant window in a city filled with horror
Outside men with stovepipe hats follow one another at regular intervals
Like the rains I loved
When the weather was fine

"The Wrath of God" was the name of the cabaret I entered last night
It was written on the white façade in even whiter letters
But the mermaids gliding behind the windows
Are too happy to be afraid
Never bodies here always the assassin without proof
Never the sky always the silence
Never freedom but for freedom

CA. 1931 • PA

AFTER THE GIANT ANTEATER

Women's stockings sift the London light*
The quays are stations black with crowds but white with vanished
    generations
And when I say London it's for poetic form
But the women's stockings are really clock hands
Beneath black mother-of-pearl garters
They belong to something I cannot name
For want of a creature who would be distinct enough from creation
And destruction to lower her own night over my thought spinning
    round
They have been carried into time by space
By female space very different from the other kind and that's all
Above the stockings is flesh and on either side of that flesh are bulldogs
Black and white as I said
And still higher the languid game that plays with a handkerchief
Everyone in a circle
And neither higher nor lower the enchanted telegraph wires
Scents confined in vague saucers
There is also a prison that brushes against the air of freedom
This contact engenders the somber flower of passion
That shatters everything in its wake with its fingers of glass

---

Untranslatable pun: the verb tamiser *(to sift) calls to mind* la Tamise,
or the Thames—thus introducing London "for poetic form."

That absorbs the ambient air the breathable air bubble by bubble
And at that elevation perennial strawberries
Are harvested morning and night in the embers
That open onto pleasure in an agate star
The armor here shows so charming a flaw
Such old earth with its pink crust becomes desirable
That words leap over the cliffs with all their roots shining
And seek the tenderest part of the ear
The electric grass has momentarily lain down
The light deflects even the ash of the eye
That remains open as if before the impossible
This flower that would be the morning-and-evening-glory
Strength and weakness drop their equipment nearby
And already the amazing feats begin
Then the dagger-colored dramas the comedies shaped like scarves
Rise by one note
And far away in the woods the future between two branches
Begins to quiver like the unappeasable absence of a leaf
Here the two pans of the scale the two sides of the hearth
Take turns submitting to the deprivation of evaluating and seeing
I think of the Great Bear but it is not she
I would like minors to understand me
And ivy to heed what I'm saying
The abrupt line the treacherous gap of fire that uncovers its face
Will be but a call of the devil in the abstract city
Toward the unswearable reign of the crackling
Nameless woman
Who smashes the jewel of this day into a thousand shards

20 MAY 1931 · MP

FREE UNION

My wife whose hair is a brush fire
Whose thoughts are summer lightning
Whose waist is an hourglass
Whose waist is the waist of an otter caught in the teeth of a tiger
Whose mouth is a bright cockade with the fragrance of a star of the
    first magnitude
Whose teeth leave prints like the tracks of white mice over snow
Whose tongue is made out of amber and polished glass
Whose tongue is a stabbed wafer
The tongue of a doll with eyes that open and shut
Whose tongue is incredible stone
My wife whose eyelashes are strokes in the handwriting of a child
Whose eyebrows are nests of swallows
My wife whose temples are the slate of greenhouse roofs
With steam on the windows
My wife whose shoulders are champagne
Are fountains that curl from the heads of dolphins under the ice
My wife whose wrists are matches
Whose fingers are raffles holding the ace of hearts
Whose fingers are fresh cut hay
My wife with the armpits of martens and beech fruit

And Midsummer Night

That are hedges of privet and nesting places for sea snails

Whose arms are of sea foam and a landlocked sea

And a fusion of wheat and a mill

Whose legs are spindles

In the delicate movements of watches and despair

My wife whose calves are sweet with the sap of elders

Whose feet are carved initials

Keyrings and the feet of steeplejacks who drink

My wife whose neck is fine milled barley

Whose throat contains the Valley of Gold

And encounters in the bed of the maelstrom

My wife whose breasts are of the night

And are undersea molehills

And crucibles of rubies

My wife whose breasts are haunted by the ghosts of dew-moistened roses

Whose belly is a fan unfolded in the sunlight

Is a giant talon

My wife with the back of a bird in vertical flight

With a back of quicksilver

And bright lights

My wife whose nape is of smooth worn stone and wet chalk

And of a glass slipped through the fingers of someone who has
    just drunk

My wife with the thighs of a skiff

That are lustrous and feathered like arrows

Stemmed with the light tailbones of a white peacock

And imperceptible balance

My wife whose rump is sandstone and flax

Whose rump is the back of a swan and the spring

My wife with the sex of an iris
A mine and a platypus
With the sex of an alga and old-fashioned candies
My wife with the sex of a mirror
My wife with eyes full of tears
With eyes that are purple armor and a magnetized needle
With eyes of savannahs
With eyes full of water to drink in prisons
My wife with eyes that are forests forever under the ax
My wife with eyes that are the equal of water and air and earth and fire

21 MAY 1931 • DA

CURTAIN CURTAIN

The traveling theaters of the seasons that played my life
While I booed
The proscenium had been converted into a prison cell from which
    I could hiss
With my hands on the bars I saw a backdrop of dark green
The heroine naked to the waist
Who committed suicide at the beginning of the first act
Inexplicably the play continued in the chandelier
Little by little the stage filled with fog
And sometimes I cried out
I broke the pitcher they had given me from which butterflies escaped
And rose madly towards the chandelier
Under the pretext of another ballet interlude of my thoughts that they
    insisted on performing for me
I then tried to slash my wrist with bits of brown earth
But these were lands in which I got lost
Impossible to pick up the thread of these travels
I was separated from everything by the bread of the sun
A character moved around the theater the only active character
Who had made himself a mask with my features
Hatefully he took the side of the ingenue and the traitor

The rumor was that it had been organized as easy as one two three
Suddenly the cave grew deeper
In the endless corridors bouquets held hand-high
Wandered alone I hardly dared to open my door a crack
All at once too much freedom had been given to me
The freedom to run away in a sleigh from my bed
The freedom to bring back to life the beings that I missed
Aluminum chairs were closing in around a kiosk of mirrors
Over which rose a curtain of dew fringed with blood that had
    turned green
The freedom to chase away the real apparitions before me
The basement was marvelous on a white wall my silhouette
    appeared in fiery dots pierced through the heart by a bullet

CA. 1931 · BZ & ZR

VIGILANCE

In Paris the Saint-Jacques Tower tottering
Like a sunflower
Sometimes bumps its forehead against the Seine and its shadow glides
    imperceptibly among the tugboats
At that moment on tiptoe in my sleep
I head for the room where I am lying
And I set it on fire
So that nothing survives of the consent torn from me
Then the furniture makes room for animals of the same size that watch
    me like a brother
Lions in whose manes the chairs are finally burnt up
Dogfish whose white bellies blend with the last shiver of the bedsheets
At the hour of love and blue eyelids
Next I see myself burning I see that solemn hiding-place of nothings
That was my body
Raked by the patient beaks of the ibises of the fire
When it's all over invisible I board the ark
Without noticing life's pedestrians who make their shuffling steps echo
    far away
I see the fishbones of the sun
Through the hawthorn of the rain

I hear the human linen being torn like a great leaf
Beneath the fingernail of absence and presence which are in alliance
All the looms fade nothing's left of them but a perfumed piece of lace
A seashell of lace in the perfect shape of a breast
All I touch is the heart of things I hold the thread

CA. 1931 · BZ & ZR

A BRANCH OF NETTLE
ENTERS THROUGH THE WINDOW

The woman with the crepe paper body
The red fish in the fireplace
Whose memory is pieced together from a multitude of small watering
    places for distant ships
Who laughs like an ember fit to be set in snow
And sees the night expand and contract like an accordion
The armor of the grass
Hilt of the dagger gate
Falling in flakes from the wings of the sphinx
Rolling the floor of the Danube
For which time and space destroy themselves
On the evening when the watchman of the inner eye trembles
    like an elf
Isn't this the stake of the battle to which my dreams surrender
Brittle bird
Rocked by the telegraph wires of trance
Shattering in the great lake created by the numbers of its song
This is the double heart of the lost wall
Gripped by grasshoppers of the blood
That drag my likeness through the mirror

My broken hands
My caterpillar eyes
My long whalebone hairs
Whalebone sealed under brilliant black wax

CA. 1931 · DA

LETHAL RELIEF

The statue of Lautréamont
Its plinth of quinine tabloids
In the open country
The author of the Poetical Works lies flat on his face
And near at hand the hiloderm a shady customer keeps vigil
His left ear is glued to the ground it is a glass case it contains
A prong of lightning the artist has not failed to figure aloft
In the form of a Turk's head the blue balloon
The Swan of Montevideo with wings unfurled ready to flap at a
    moment's notice
Should the problem of luring the other swans from the horizon arise
Opens upon the false universe two eyes of different hues
The one of sulphate of iron on vines of the lashes the other of
    sparkling mire
He beholds the vast funnelled hexagon where now in no time
    the machines
By man in dressings rabidly swaddled
Shall lie a-writhing
With his radium bougie he quickens the dregs of the human crucible
With his sex of feathers and his brain of bull-paper

He presides at the twice nocturnal ceremonies whose object due
    allowance for fire having been made is the interversion of the
    hearts of the bird and the man
Convulsionary in ordinary I have access to his side
The ravishing women who introduce me into the rose-padded
    compartment
Where a hammock that they have been at pains to contrive with
    their tresses for
Me is reserved for
Me for all eternity
Exhort me before taking their departure not to catch a chill in the
    perusal of the daily
It transpires that the statue in whose latitude the squitch of my
    nerve terminals
Weighs anchor is tuned each night like a piano

5 APRIL 1932 · SB

IN THE LOVELY
HALF-LIGHT OF 1934 . . .

In the lovely half-light of 1934
The air was a splendid rosey hue the color of red mullet
And the forest when I first entered it
Began with a tree covered with cigarette-paper leaves
Since I was waiting for you
And since anytime you walk with me
Anywhere at all
Your mouth turns so happily into the enamel tip of an axle-tree
Around which a ceaselessly ascending diffuse blue broken wheel
    of words revolves
Paling now and then in roadside ruts
Alluring wonders rushed over to greet me
A squirrel pressed its white belly against my heart
I've no idea how he remained poised there
For the earth was awash with reflections even deeper than those
    in water
As if metal had finally split its shell
And you who were lying prone stretched out on a terrifying sea
    of jewelry
Turned

Naked

Like a sunful of skyrockets

I saw you slowly removing from among the radiolarians

The empty shell of the sea-urchin I'd been

But wait I wasn't there anymore

I was casting my eyes to the skies because already my living casket
 of white velvet had abandoned me

And I was sad

The sky between the leaves shone haggard and hard as a dragonfly

And I was just about to close both my eyes

When two wooden blinders which had flown apart suddenly
 snapped shut once again

Without a sound

Like the two innermost leaves of an immense Lily of the Valley

A flower able to contain the entire night

So I was there where you see me still

Amid perfumes chiming out in great pealing waves

But before they could spring open once again as each day they do
 in this changing life

I had just enough time to fasten my lips

Firmly on your glass thighs

1934 · MB

IT WAS GOING ON
FIVE IN THE MORNING . . .

It was going on five in the morning
The ship of steam stretched its chain to shatter the windows
And outside
A glowworm
Lifted Paris like a leaf
It was only a long trembling scream
A scream from the Maternity Hospital nearby
FINIS FOUNDRY FANATIC
But whatever joy escaped in the exhalation of that pain
It seems to me that I was falling for a long time
I still had my fist clenched around a handful of grass
And suddenly that rustle of flowers and needles of ice
Those green eyebrows that shooting-star pendulum
From what depths was the bell actually able to rise again
The hermetic bell
Which nothing last night made me foresee would stop on this landing
The bell whose sides read
Undine
Moving to raise your spearheaded Sagittarius pedal

You had carved the infallible signs
Of my enchantment
With a dagger whose coral handle forks into infinity
So that your blood and mine
Would become one

1934 • BZ & ZR

Always for the first time
As if I hardly know what you look like
You come back at a certain time of night to a house at an angle to
    my window
A completely imaginary house
Where from one second to the next
In the unbroken darkness
I expect it to happen again the fascinating ripping
The one and only ripping
Of its façade and my heart
The closer I come to you
In reality
The more the key sings in the door of the unknown room
Where you appear for me all alone
First you are totally fused with the brightness
The fleeting angle of a curtain
It's a field of jasmine I've gazed on at dawn on a road just outside Grasse
With its diagonal of women pickers
Behind them the shadowy falling wing of stripped seedlings
In front of them the T-square of dazzlement
The curtain invisibly raised

All the flowers come back in a tumult

It's you in the grip of this long long hour never troubled enough
    till you fall asleep

You as though you could be

The same except that maybe I'll never meet you

You pretend not to know I watch you

Amazingly I'm no longer sure you know it

Your idleness brings tears to my eyes

A cloud of interpretations surrounds each of your movements

It's a hunt for honeydew

There are rocking chairs on a bridge there are branches trying to
    scratch you in the forest

In a shop window on the Rue Notre-Dame-de-Lorette there are

Two beautiful crossed legs trapped in long stockings

That flare out at the center of a big white clover

There's

Only for me to lean over the cliff

Of the hopeless fusion of your presence and your absence

I've discovered the secret

Of always loving you

For the first time

1934 · BZ & ZR

FULL MARGIN

for Pierre Mabille

I am not one for followers
I've never lived in the place called La Grenouillère
The oil lamp of my heart leaks and sputters when approaching a
    churchyard

I have never been drawn but toward things that don't go gentle
The tree chosen by the storm
The ship of lights brought to berth by a ship's boy
The edifice viewed only by the unblinking lizard and a thousand vines

I have only seen to the exclusion of all others women who took issue
    with their times
Or else they rose toward me lifted by vapors of the abyss

Or else absent less than a second ago they preceded me to the step of
    the Dulcimer Player
In the all but windless street where their hair brandished the torch

And above all that queen of Byzantium whose eyes reach so far
    beyond ultramarine
That I can never find myself in the neighborhood of Les Halles where
    she appeared to me
Without her multiplying endlessly in the windowed stalls of violet sellers

Above all the child of the caverns her embrace prolonging for life the
    Eskimo night
When already breathless daybreak etches its antlers on the window

Above all the nun with nasturtium lips
In the bus from Crozon to Quimper
The sound of her eyelashes disturbs the coal-tit
And the book with its clasp will slip from her folded legs

Above all the ancient winged guardian of the Portal
Through which conjectures dodge among the rickshaws
She shows me stalls full of ideographic inscriptions lined up along
    the Seine
She is standing on a broken lotus egg beside my ear

Above all she who smiles at me from the depths of Berre pond
When from a bridge in Martigues pressed against me she happens
    to follow the slow parade of setting lamps
The jellyfish in ball gowns twirling in the lights
She who feigns not to be the cause of this celebration
Not to know that this accompaniment repeated each day back and forth
Is votive

Above all

I come back to my wolves my ways of feeling
True luxury
Is that the white satin padded sofa
Wears a star of laceration

I need these evening glories obliquely hitting your laurel woods

The giant seashells of erected systems rising in irregular sections
    from the countryside
With their pearly staircases and reflections like old lantern glass
Hold my attention only because of the giddiness
They've inspired in man who sometimes went so far as to break the
    foot pedals
Rather than let the great rumbling escape

I take my pleasure in the cracks in rocks where the sea
Throws its globes of horses ridden by howling dogs
Where consciousness is no longer bread in its kingly robe
But a kiss the only one recharged by its own embers

And even those who took a path that isn't my own
That could easily be mistaken for the opposite of my own
At first it gets obscured by the fable of origins
But the wind kicks up fast the handrails twist crazily around their
    iridescent knobs
And for them the universe flew out the window
No longer watching for what should never end

Day and night exchange their pledges
Or lovers out of time finding and losing the ring of their source

O great palpable movement by which others finally become mine
Even they in life's burst of laughter framed by a monk's cowl
They whose looks open a red breach in the brambles
Carry me carry me where I do not know to follow
Eyes blindfolded you're burning up you're getting colder getting
    colder
However they came to knock there's always a place set for them at
    my table

My handsome Pelagius crowned with mistletoe your head erect over
    all those bent brows

Joachim of Floris led by terrible angels
Who still today at certain hours fold their wings above the boulevards
Where chimneys burst forth inviting us to a resolution in tenderness
    nearer
Than Giotto's heptagonal pink constructions

Meister Eckhardt my master at the inn of reason
Where Hegel told Novalis With him we have everything we need
    and off they went
With them and the wind I have everything I need

Jansen yes I was waiting for you prince of rigor
You must be cold

The only one who in his lifetime managed to be his own shadow
And from his dust they saw the spasm flower rise threatening the
    entire city
Deacon Paris

The beautiful violated humble overwhelming Cadière

And you the brothers Bonjour
Who with great pomp and circumstance have gone and crucified
    two women I believe
You of whom an old peasant from Fareins-en-Dôle
At home amid portraits of Marat and Mother Angélique
Told me that in disappearing you left for those who have come or
    who might come
Enough to last a long while

SALON-MARTIGUES; SEPTEMBER 1940 · MP

from FATA MORGANA

[...]
The bed hurtles down rails of blue honey
Freeing into transparency animals from medieval sculpture
It tips and nearly spills onto the slopes of foxglove
And is lit in flashes by the eyes of birds of prey
Loaded with all the emanations from Otranto's giant feathered helmet
The bed hurtles down rails of blue honey
It tries to outrun the changeable skies
That are always in season the spikes of park fences rising
And thickening smoke follows the dancers climbing onto the countertop
The bed shoots past the signals it blurs all the goldfish bowls into one
It tries to outrun the changeable skies
Nothing in common you know with the little railroad
That coils through Cordoba Mexico so that we never tired of discovering
The scent-laden gardenias in the hollow shoots of palm trees
Or elsewhere to allow us to choose
From the train door among the batches of uncut opals and turquoise
No the bed trailing its crazy filament does not stop at unrolling the silk
    of incomparable places and days
It is the loom where cycles cross and from which bursts what we sense
    as music of the spheres

The bed shoots past the signals it blurs all the goldfish bowls into one
And when it digs whistling into the carnal tunnel
The walls fall away the old golden dust rises blindingly from civil
    registers
Finally all is reclaimed by the movement of the sea
No the bed trailing its crazy filament does not stop at unrolling the
    silk of incomparable places and days
It's the play with no intermission the curtain raised once and for all
    on the cascade
Tell me
How to protect ourselves in transit from the pernicious afterthought
That we're not going where we wish
The little square receding in the distance and lined with trees that
    are imperceptibly different from every other tree
Exists for us to pass through in real life at a given angle
The stream in this very curve as in no other curve among all streams
Is master of a secret that it cannot make ours just in passing
Behind the window the faintly lit one among so many others
    variously lit
What *happens*
Is of the utmost importance to us perhaps we should return
Have the courage to knock
Who says they wouldn't welcome us with open arms
But nothing is certain everyone is afraid we ourselves
Are nearly as afraid
And still I'm sure that deep in the woods under lock and key
    turning now against the windowpane
A single clearing opens
Is that love the promise that surpasses us
That eternal round-trip ticket modeled on the variegated moth

Is it love those fingers squeezing the husk of the mist
So that out will spring unknown cities with sadly fabulous doors
Love is those telegraph wires that turn the insatiable light into a
    jewel endlessly opening
Cut to the size of our nighttime compartment
You come to me from beyond the shadows I won't say in the space
    of thousand-year-old sequoias
Into your voice climb the trills of lost birds

Lovely loaded dice
Fortune and misfortune
At the cardsharp's table all those wide-eyed stares around an open
    umbrella
What revenge the fortune teller's good-luck charm
My hand closes on her
If I could escape my fate

We must drive away the old blind man from the lichens on the
    church wall
Destroy every last one of those horrible pamphlets in faded yellow
    green blue pink
Decorated with a variable and bloodless flower
That he invites you to pull off his chest
One by one for just a few cents

But strength always remains
In the ancient tongue the simple ones the cauldron
A mane of hair appearing in the fire
And no matter what we do never hoisted onto the heart of all light
The pirate flag

A tall man treading a perilous road
Was not content to slip the steel-tipped armbands of a famous criminal
  beneath his workman's coveralls
To his right the lion in his hand the sea urchin
He heads east
Where already the woodgrouse swells the bilberries with vapor and
  muffled sounds
Here he is trying to ford the torrent the stones which are gleams from the
  shoulders of women in box seats
Pivoting very slowly and in vain
I had lost sight of him he reappears a bit farther down on the other bank
Checks that he is still carrying the sea urchin
The lion to his right all right
The soil that he barely grazes crackles with the debris of scythes

Meanwhile that man rushes down a staircase in the heart of a city he has
  cast aside his armor
Outside they're fighting against what cannot last
This man among so many others who are suddenly alike
What is *he what more than himself can he be feeling*
So that what cannot last
                    does not last
He is quite prepared not to last himself
One for all come what may
Or life might be the drop of poison
Of nonsense introduced into the meadowlark's song above the poppies
The storm passes

Meanwhile
That man who collected traps around the lighthouse

Hesitates to go home he carefully lifts seaweed and more seaweed
The wind has died so be it
And still more seaweed that he lays back down
As if forbidden to uncover fully the most secret body of the young woman
From which a winged contraption rises
Here the weather simultaneously clouds over and brightens
From the trapeze all made of cicadas
A very little girl asks mysteriously
André don't you know why I repetunia
All at once a pyramid looms in the distance
To life and death what is beginning precedes me and finishes me off
A fine stone openwork pyramid
Bound to that lovely body with vermilion laces
[...]

DECEMBER 1940 • MP

WAR

for Max Ernst

I watch the Beast as it licks itself
The better to confound itself with all that surrounds it
Its storm-colored eyes
Are unexpectedly the pond dragging to itself the filthy linen the rubbish
The one that always stops man
The pond with its little Place de l'Opéra in its belly
Because phosphorescence is the key to the eyes of the Beast
That licks itself
And its tongue
Thrust one never knows beforehand in what direction
Is a crossroad of braziers
From below I contemplate its palate
Made of lamps in bags
And beneath the royal blue vault
Of ungilded arches set in perspective one within the other
While blows the breath made of the infinite generalization of that of
    one of those bare-chested wretches who appear in public squares
    swallowing gasoline torches in an acrid shower of pennies

The pustules of the Beast grow resplendent in those hecatombs of
	young men on which the Number gorges
With its flanks protected by the shimmering scales that are armies
All domed and each of them turning perfectly on its hinge
Although they all depend on one another no less than cocks that insult
	each other from dungheap to dungheap
One touches the flaw of conscience yet some persist in arguing that day
	will break
The door I wanted to say the Beast licks itself beneath its wing
And one sees crooks shaken is it with laughter at the back of a tavern
That mirage that they have made out to be the good is open to discussion
It is a bed of quicksilver
It could be lapped up all at one go
I thought the Beast was turning towards me I saw again the filth of the
	lightning
How white it is in its membranes in the looseness of its white birchwoods
	where they keep watch
In the ropes of its ships at whose prow a woman dives who has been
	adorned with a green harlequin mask by the toils of love
False alarm the Beast keeps its claws in an erectile crown around its
	nipples
I try not to be too unsteady when it stirs its tail
That is at the same time the bevelled carriage and the whiplash
In the suffocating odor of tiger-beetles
From its lair befouled with black blood and gold towards the moon it
	sharpens one of its horns on the enthusiastic tree of grudges
It coils itself with frightening languors
Petted
The Beast licks its sex I said nothing

CA. 1941 • ER

DREAMS

But the light returns
the pleasure of smoking
The spider-fairy of the cinders in points of blue and red
is never content with her mansions of Mozart.
The wound heals everything uses its ingenuity to make itself
recognized I speak and beneath your face the cone of shadow
turns which from the depths of the sea has called the pearls
the eyelids, the lips, inhale the day
the arena empties itself
one of the birds in flying away
did not think to forget the straw and the thread
hardly has a crowd thought it fit to stir
when the arrow flies
a star nothing but a star lost in the fur of the night

NEW YORK; OCTOBER 1943 • RD

KORWAR

You hold on like no other
You were caught as you came out of life
To re-enter it
I don't know if it's in one direction or in another that you shake the
    garden gate
You have raised up to your heart the serpentine grass
And forever curled the birds of paradise in the hoarse sky
Your gaze is clairvoyant
You are seated
And we too are seated
The skull for a few more days
In the dip of our features
All our acts are before us
At arm's length
In the little ones' vine tendril
You are feeding us a line on existentialism
There are no flies on you

CA. 1947 • MAC & JPC

RANO RARAKU

How lovely the world is
Greece never existed
They shall not pass
My horse finds his peck in the crater
Birdmen curved swimmers
Flit around my head for
I too
Am there
Three quarters bogged down
Kidding some ethnologists
In the friendly Southern night
They shall not pass
The plain is immense
Those who move forward are ridiculous
The high images are fallen

CA. 1947 • MAC & JPC

ON THE ROAD TO SAN ROMANO

Poetry is made in bed like love
Its unmade sheets are the dawn of things
Poetry is made in a forest

She has the space which she needs
Not this one but the other

    Governed by the hawk's eye
    The dew on the spindle
    The memory of a moist bottle of Traminer on a silver platter
    A tall rod of tourmaline over the sea
    A road of mental adventure
    Which climbs abruptly
    One pause and it's instantly overgrown

Don't shout that from the roof tops
It's not fitting to leave the doors open
Or go around calling for witnesses

The shoals of fishes the hedges of small birds
The rails at the approach to the great station
The glow of two river banks
The furrows on a loaf of bread
Bubbles in a brook
The days of the calendar
Hog-wart

The act of love and the act of poetry
Are incompatible
With reading newspapers at the top of one's voice

The way the sunlight falls
The livid glitter which binds the ax-strokes of the woodcutter
The string of a kite in the shape of a heart or a fish-trap
The steady waving of the beaver's tail
The perseverance of lightning
The flinging down of sweets from the top of an old staircase
An avalanche

The room of marvels
No gentlemen not the forbidden chamber
Nor the fumes of the barracks room on Sunday evenings

The figure of the dance executed transparently above the marshes
The body of a woman outlined by throwing knives
The lucent rings of smoke
The curls of your hair
The twisting of a sponge from the Philippines

The snakelike coils of coral
The ivy's slitherings into the ruins
She has all of time ahead of her

The embrace of poetry like the embrace of the naked body
Protects while it lasts
Against all access by the misery of the world

1948 • CS & MB

ON THE ROAD TO SAN ROMANO

[VERSION 2]

Poetry like love is made in a bed.
In her messed-up sheets the sun rises.
Poetry lives in deep woods.

She has all the room she needs.

One whole side of the universe

> Is ruled by a hawk's gaze,
> By the dewdrop on a furled fern,
> By the memory of a sweating bottle of Fumé Blanc on a silver tray,
> By a thin blue vein down an obelisk poised over the sea.
> And the road of mental adventure, which peaks abruptly—
> One pause and it's weeded over.

No need to spread this around.
Wouldn't want to frighten the horses.

> Shoals of salmon, hedges of songbirds,
> Rail-flanks opening before the approach of a railhead,

Reflections from two banks of a river,
The valleys baked into a loaf,
The odd and even days of the calendar.

The act of love and the act of poetry
Are incompatible
With reading the news at the top of one's voice.

The way the sun shines,
The blue blur that binds the arc of the woodsman's axe—
The reach of a kite string,
The measured beating of a beaver's tail,
The diligence of lightning,
Someone tossing candies down from the top of an old staircase.

A good address is not necessarily part of the action—
Nor a corner office.
No, gentlemen—nor gin, leather, and cigar smoke.

Dance steps footed on a summer's night,
The shape of a woman's body delineated by throwing-knives,
Blown ephemeral smoke-rings,
The curls of your hair,
Slippery flutters of wettest flesh,
Ivy slithering into ruins.

The embrace of poetry,
Like love's impossible, perfect fit,
Defends while it lasts
Against all the misery of the world.

1948 · RT

LE LA

O^3 whose skin-snapping lives in C major like an average.
Night of 27 to 28 October 1951.

The moon begins where the cherry finishes with the lemon.
Night of 6 to 7 February 1953.

Then they'll compose a newspaper whose complicated,
nervous signature will be a nickname.
Night of 11 to 12 May 1953.

If you live gold white bison, don't trim gold white bison.
Night of 11 to 12 April 1956.

1961 • BZ & MP

SUBJECT

for Jean Paulhan

May I, with the help of God, become hardened someday. For months they have put me in such a sorry position! Can the *maintenance* of a man so wholly usurp everyone's attention? Capable of the highest degree of devotion to society, I was of course designated as the experimenter's choice. Even today, were they to convince me, I might still make a sacrifice of my reason to the human race. But the purpose of your maneuvers escapes me. Apparently you'll stick at nothing to succeed. I am dwarfed by the scale of your stage directions.

You claim it's war, while official notices and train announcements take their places to further the illusion. The bit players in stations act out their simulated farewells, but I wager that the moment I turn my back on the performance they return to hearth and home. That made-to-order emulation: a spectacular trial never happened—if Jaurès himself appeared before me I wouldn't mistake him for his ghost. These are indeed perilous times for Paris. I go deaf the moment they try to make me hear between the lines; my calm must stupefy them. The large-circulation dailies seem so anxious for me to bare my heart and soul. You have to see how their communiqués, losing all sense of measure, take such pains to rouse my passion.

Hero, miracle: they now essay the power of magic words. This deserves better than the declarations of refugees. I must protest your tactless demand for my thanksgiving. A rare discernment makes me sensitive to all your faults. Otherwise, I bend under the yoke: at the first headstrong impulse they talk about bloody repression. A melancholy has just made me the Isolated One without Baggage or Horses. What good would my refusal serve?—Exploring the so-called kill zone, I make a game of showing up the deception for what it is.

Death is too paltry a bugaboo for me to seek the darkness of shelters. I am at least a head taller than those trenches. "Volunteer for all dangerous missions," in the words of my citation, I practically give away the spectacle of my exemplary bravery.

They appear quite satisfied. I'm entitled to some rest. Haven't I shown, by my total consent to sacrifice my life—you may take my word for it—just how *civilized* I am? This August 21, during an unprecedented bombardment, I intentionally exposed myself in open terrain, conducting the passing shells with my finger. And how charming the torpedoes were. I brushed them aside; they refreshed the air to increase the sales of those lovely ladies who rush up holding them in their arms: "Breeze, 1917 Style." Dazed by gypsies, lost among the footlights, a waltzer sometimes fell, clasping a hand to his vermilion rose. With such artifice, they have so far held me in the grip of the sublime, although the apparatus of death did not impress me the way they believed. I stepped over some corpses, it's true. They furnish the dissection rooms with them. A good many more might have been made of wax. Most of the "wounded" appeared quite content. As for the illusion of spilt blood, it has a part to play even in the provinces, thanks to the theatrical works of M. Dumas. And don't bandages conceal all their indiscretions? My quartermaster has a huge scab on his face, but he probably just met someone's fist. How much does it cost to make an entire company disappear, little by little?

CA. 1917 • MP

THE NEW SPIRIT

On Monday, 16 January, at 5:10 P.M., Louis Aragon was walking up Rue Bonaparte when he saw coming toward him a young woman in a tan-and-brown plaid tailored suit, wearing a cap made from the same fabric as her dress. She seemed to be very cold, despite the relatively mild temperature. Thanks to the light coming from the bookstore Le Coq, Aragon noted that she was of uncommon beauty and in particular that her eyes were huge. He wanted to go talk to her but remembered that he was carrying only two francs and twenty centimes. He was still thinking about her when André Breton joined him at the Deux Magots café. "I've just had an extraordinary encounter," said the latter the moment he sat down. "Walking up Rue Bonaparte, I passed a young woman who kept glancing over her shoulder, even though she seemed not to be waiting for anyone. A little before Rue Jacob she pretended to be absorbed in the display window of the prints shop, until an unbelievable, utterly vile passerby who had noticed her engaged her in conversation. They took a few steps together and stopped to talk, while I stood watching some distance away. Soon they parted, and the woman seemed to be even more disoriented. She retraced her steps for a moment; then, spotting a rather mediocre-looking character crossing the street, she suddenly went up to him. A few seconds later they dove into the Clichy-Odéon bus. I wasn't able to catch up to them. I noticed that they stayed on the rear platform, while a bit farther up the street the fat man from before was standing still, as if filled with remorse."

Aragon, as we said, seemed especially to have been struck by the stranger's beauty; Breton, by her very proper attire, her "young girl just getting out of school" aspect, with something extraordinarily *lost* in her bearing. Was she on drugs? Had she just suffered a tragedy? Aragon and Breton had great difficulty understanding the passionate interest they both took in this failed adventure. The latter was certain that, although he had seen the woman leave on the bus, she was still at the same place on Rue Bonaparte. He wanted to be sure. Walking out of the café he met André Derain, who promised to join him there in a few minutes.

"I've come back empty-handed," Breton told Aragon soon afterward. Neither one could get over his disappointment and, when Derain showed up, they couldn't help telling him the reason for their upset. They had no sooner begun than Derain cut them off: "A plaid suit," he cried. "But I just saw her near the fence at Saint-Germain-des-Prés. She was with a black man. He was laughing, and I even heard him say, 'Something will have to change.' Before that I'd seen this woman from a distance stopping other people, and for a moment I'd even expected her to come talk to me. I'm sure I've never seen her around here before, though I know every hooker in the neighborhood."

At six o'clock Louis Aragon and André Breton, unable to give up the idea of finding the key to the riddle, searched through part of the sixth arrondissement—but in vain.

1922 · MP

from THE DISDAINFUL CONFESSION

[...] To those who, on the strength of currently fashionable theories, would try to determine what emotional trauma might have turned me into a person who could say such things, I can do no less, before concluding, than dedicate the following portrait, which they can insert into the slim volume of *Letters from the Front* by Jacques Vaché, published in 1918 by Au Sans Pareil. I'm sure that the few facts this portrait helps to reconstruct will illustrate quite nicely the little I have said. It is still very hard to define just what Jacques Vaché meant by "umor" (no *h*) and to clarify where we stand with regard to the battle he waged between his capacity for emotion and certain impassive aspects of his character. There will be time later for confronting umor with the kind of poetry that, ultimately, can do without poems: that is, poetry in the sense we understand it. For the moment I will limit myself to relating a few vivid memories.

It was in Nantes, where, in early 1916, I was stationed as a temporary intern at the neurological center, that I first met Jacques Vaché. At the time he was being treated at the hospital on Rue du Boccage for a leg wound. One year older than I, he was a very elegant young man with red hair who had studied with Luc-Olivier Merson at the Ecole des Beaux-Arts. Confined to his bed, he passed the time by drawing and painting a series of postcards, for which he thought up outlandish captions. Men's fashions occupied the bulk of his imagination. He loved the clean-shaven faces and hieratic attitudes you see in bars. Every morning he spent a good hour laying out one or two photographs, a few goblets, and some violets on a small, lace-covered table, just within reach. Back then I was composing poems in the style of Mallarmé. I was going through one of the most difficult periods of my life, beginning to see that I would not be able to do what I wanted. The war dragged on. Auxiliary hospital no. 103-*bis* echoed with the shouts of the doctor on call—a charming fellow, moreover: "Dyspepsia? never heard of it. There are two kinds of stomach ailments: one is certainly cancer; the other, though doubtful, is ulcers. Give him two helpings of meat and salad and he'll get over it. I'll be your death, friend," and so on. Jacques Vaché smiled. We spoke of Rimbaud (whom he had always hated), Apollinaire (with whom he was barely familiar), Jarry (whom he admired), Cubism (which he distrusted). He was stingy with information about his past. I believe that he reproached in me my will toward art and modernism, which since that time … but let's not get ahead of ourselves. His attitude bore no trace of snobbery. "Dada" did not exist yet, and Jacques Vaché would never know about it. Consequently, it was he who first insisted on the importance of gestures, which are so dear to Mr. André Gide. The condition of being a soldier is particularly suited to personal effusiveness. Someone who has never been forced to snap to attention cannot know how badly you can long to take to your heels. Jacques Vaché was a past master in the art of "attaching very little importance to anything." He understood that sentimentality was no longer the order of the day and that a proper regard for one's dignity, whose fundamental value hadn't yet been underscored by Charlie Chaplin, required a certain impassiveness. "We needed our air dry, a little," he writes in his letters. In 1916 one barely had time to recognize a friend. Even *behind the lines* meant nothing. All that mattered was to keep living, and the simple fact of polishing rings in the trenches* or turning one's head struck us as corrupt. Writing and thinking were no longer enough; above all, one had to cultivate the illusion of movement, of noise.

Scarcely out of the hospital, Jacques Vaché got himself hired as a stevedore and unloaded coal from the Loire. He spent his afternoons in the slums near the port. In the evening he went from café to café, movie house to movie house, dropping inordinate sums of money, creating around himself an atmosphere at once dramatic and vivid, spun from the lies he liked to tell (he introduced me to everyone as André Salmon, because of the minor reputation this writer enjoyed—which I didn't fully appreciate until later). I have to admit that he did not share my enthusiasms and that for a long time he saw me as the "powet," someone who hadn't fully absorbed the lesson of the times. He *occasionally* strolled around Nantes in the uniform of a lieutenant in the hussards, or of an airman, or a doctor. It might be that, meeting you on the street, he would pretend not to recognize you and would continue on his way without a backward glance. Vaché never shook hands, to say either hello or goodbye. He lived in Place du Beffroi, in a pretty room with a young woman whom I knew only as Louise and whom, when I visited, he obliged to sit still and silent for hours in a corner. At five o'clock she served tea, and his only thanks was to kiss her hand. As he told it, they had no sexual relations; rather, he was content simply to sleep beside her in the same bed. This was, he assured me, his standard practice. Still, he seemed to like calling her "my mistress," no doubt anticipating the question that Gide would later ask: "Was Jacques Vaché a virgin?"

*An allusion to Apollinaire's poem "The Seasons" (in *Calligrammes*), in which he recounts "polishing till evening incredible rings" in the trenches. (Trans.)

Starting in May 1916 I was to see my friend only five or six more times. He had been sent back to the front, from where he would write me sporadically (he who wrote to no one, except, out of self-interest, to his mother every two or three months). On 23 June 1917, returning at around two in the morning to La Pitié hospital, where I was being treated, I found a note from him, along with the drawing that figures as the frontispiece of his *Letters*. He set a date for the following afternoon at the premiere of *Les Mamelles de Tirésias*.

It was at the Conservatoire Maubel that I next saw Jacques Vaché. The first act had just ended. A British officer was making a scene in the orchestra seats: it could only have been he. The ruckus surrounding the performance had excited him tremendously. He had gone into the theater revolver in hand and spoke of firing on the audience. To tell the truth, Apollinaire's "surrealist drama" was not much to his liking; he deemed the play too literary and strongly disapproved of the costume design.

As we went out, he confided that he wasn't alone in Paris. The evening before, leaving La Pitié after hoping to find me there, he had gone for a walk and, near the Gare de Lyon, had been *fortunate enough* to rescue a "little girl" from two thugs who were manhandling her. He had taken the child under his wing; she couldn't have been more than sixteen or seventeen. What was she doing, hanging around a train station in the middle of the night? He hadn't worried about it. Because she seemed extremely tired, he had offered to take her on the train, it didn't matter where, and thus they ended up in Fontenay-aux-Roses. There they had begun to walk, and it was only at Jeanne's insistence that he had finally sought shelter for the night. It was now around four o'clock. A man putting out the streetlamps, who by a poetic co-incidence was an undertaker by day, offered them hospitality. The next day—the day of our appointment—they had gotten up late and had barely made it back to Montmartre in time. Jacques had asked the girl to wait for him in a grocery store with a few pennies' worth of candy. He was leaving me at the end of the afternoon to go join her. She was very young, apparently rather naive; he had slung his staff officer's ID card around her neck. She accompanied us to the Rat Mort, where Jacques Vaché showed me a few of his war sketches, notably some studies for a "Lafcadio." He obviously felt great tenderness for Jeanne and had promised to take her to Biarritz; in the meantime he was staying with her in a hotel near the Bastille. Needless to say, he left by himself the next day without any more of a backward glance than usual, perfectly heedless of the sacrifice that Jeanne claimed to have made for him of her life . . . and of two days on the job. I have reason to believe that in exchange she gave him a dose of syphilis.

Three months later Jacques was again in Paris. He came to see me but soon left on that beautiful morning to go walk alone by the Ourcq canal. I can still see the long traveling coat draped over his shoulders, the somber air with which he spoke of *success in the grocery business.* "You'll think I'm missing, or dead, and one day—anything's possible—" (he uttered this sort of expression in a singsong voice) "you'll learn that a certain Jacques Vaché is living in retirement in some Normandy or other. He spends his time raising livestock. He'll introduce you to his wife, a rather pretty and innocent young thing, who will never suspect the danger she was courting. Only a few books—very few, mind you—carefully locked away on the top floor will bear witness to the fact that something happened." Even this illusion would soon abandon him, as attested by his letter of 9 May 1918.

The last stage of Jacques Vaché's life is marked by his famous letter of 14 November, which all my friends know by heart: "I'll emerge from the war gently doddering, perhaps indeed like those splendid village idiots (and I hope so) . . . or else . . . or else . . . what a film I'll play in!—With insane automobiles, don't you know, and bridges that collapse, and enormous hands creeping over the screen toward some document—useless and priceless!—With such tragic conversations, in evening wear," etc.; and this delirium, more poignant for us than the deliria of *A Season in Hell:* "I'll also be a trapper, or thief, or prospector, or hunter, or miner, or well driller. Arizona Bar (whiskey, gin and mixed) and fine, high-yielding forests, and you know those beautiful riding breeches with their machine pistols, the clean-shaven look, and such lovely hands for playing solitaire. It'll all go up in smoke, I tell you, or in a saloon, having made my fortune.—Well."

Jacques Vaché killed himself in Nantes shortly after the armistice. His death was admirable in that it could pass for an accident. I believe he absorbed forty grams of opium, although, as you might well imagine, he was not an inexperienced smoker. On the other hand, it is quite possible that his unfortunate companions did not know how to use drugs and that he wanted, in disappearing, to play a final *hilarious trick* on them. [...]

1923 · MP

THREE DREAMS

I

[…] In Pantin, I am walking up Route d'Aubervilliers toward the Town Hall when, in front of a house where I once lived, I run into a funeral procession, which to my astonishment is heading not toward but away from the cemetery. I soon come abreast of the hearse. Sitting astride the casket, an extremely pale older man wearing mourning clothes and a top hat, who must be the deceased, is waving to the passers-by, turning sometimes to the left, sometimes to the right. The procession advances straight into a match factory.

I I

I arrive in Paris and walk down the stairs of a train station much like the Gare de l'Est. I feel a terrific need to urinate and go to cross the square, where I know I can get relief, when several feet away on my side of the street I discover a small-scale urinal, of a new and quite elegant model. No sooner do I reach it than I notice the urinal is mobile and, as I'm not alone here, I also realize that this mobility has its drawbacks. All in all, it's just another vehicle, and I decide to remain on the platform. From there I can see the swoops of a second "flying toilet" similar to ours, too close for comfort. Unable to draw the other passengers' attention to its erratic flight and the danger it poses to pedestrians, I jump off and persuade the careless driver to leave his seat and follow me. He's a young man, less than thirty; his replies to my questions are highly evasive. He claims to be a military doctor, and of course he has a driver's license. A stranger to the city we're in, he says he has come "from the brush," without being more specific. Doctor though he may be, I try to convince him that he himself might be ill, but the symptoms he lists for me belong to a wide variety of diseases, beginning with different fevers: symptoms with which he doesn't present, and which moreover are of the most basic clinical sort. He ends his account with the reflection, "At most, I might only be a general paralytic." [...]

| | |

Evening, at home. Picasso is ensconced in the sofa, at the corner of two walls; but this Picasso is halfway between his current state and that of his soul after death. He is sketching absently on a pad. Each page contains only a few rapid strokes and the enormous figures of the asking price: 150 francs. He barely answers me and doesn't seem to care that I found out how he spent his time in Beg-Meil, where I'd arrived shortly after his departure. The shadow of Apollinaire is also in the room, standing against the door; it seems somber, filled with troubled thoughts. It agrees to let me come out with it, though I have no idea where it's going. As we walk, I'm dying to ask it a question, a question of some importance, for want of being able to hold a real conversation. But what is it I wish to know, more than anything? No doubt it will satisfy my curiosity only once. What good would it do to ask Apollinaire what's become of his political convictions since his death, reassure myself that he's no longer such a chauvinist, etc.? After much thought, I decide to ask what he thinks of himself as we knew him, of the more or less great poet he once was. This is, I believe, the second time he has been asked about this and I hasten to apologize. Does he feel his death was premature, and can he at all enjoy his posthumous fame? "No and no." He admits that when he thinks about Apollinaire, it's as if about a stranger for whom he feels no more than a bland sympathy.

We are about to turn onto a Roman road and suddenly I think I know where the shadow is leading me (it won't take me by surprise, I'm quite proud of that). Indeed, at the far end of this road stands a house that occupies a considerable place in my life. Inside it a corpse is lying on a bed, which is bathed in a phosphorescent glow; around the bed, hallucinatory phenomena, which I have witnessed, occur at certain intervals. But we are still nowhere near, and already the shadow is pushing open the two panels of a dark red door framed by gold buttons. I get it, it's only a brothel. Unable to make it change its mind, I take my leave of the shadow with great regret and turn back. I am soon confronted by seven or eight young women, who have come away from a group to my left that I can barely make out, and who, *all four of them,* block my path with outstretched arms. They're doing their best to make me go back again. I finally manage to get rid of them by dint of compliments and promises, one more cowardly than the next.

I've now taken a seat in a train, opposite a girl in mourning who has, it seems, behaved badly, and who is being scolded by her mother. She is being offered a chance to show remorse, yet she stubbornly keeps silent.

CA. 1924 · MP

from MANIFESTO OF SURREALISM

So strong is the belief in life, in what is most fragile in life—*real* life, I mean—that in the end this belief is lost. Man, that inveterate dreamer, daily more discontent with his destiny, has trouble assessing the objects he has been led to use, objects that his nonchalance has brought his way, or that he has earned through his own efforts, almost always through his own efforts, for he has agreed to work, at least he has not refused to try his luck (or what he calls his luck!). At this point he feels extremely modest: he knows what women he has had, what silly affairs he has been involved in; he is unimpressed by his wealth or poverty, in this respect he is still a newborn babe and, as for the approval of his conscience, I confess that he does very nicely without it. If he still retains a certain lucidity, all he can do is turn back toward his childhood which, however his guides and mentors may have botched it, still strikes him as somehow charming. There, the absence of any known restrictions allows him the perspective of several lives lived at once; this illusion becomes firmly rooted within him; now he is only interested in the fleeting, the extreme facility of everything. Children set off each day without a worry in the world. Everything is near at hand, the worst material conditions are fine. The woods are white or black, one will never sleep.

But it is true that we would not dare venture so far, it is not merely a question of distance. Threat is piled upon threat, one yields, abandons a portion of the terrain to be conquered. This imagination which knows no bounds is henceforth allowed to be exercised only in strict accordance with the laws of an arbitrary utility; it is incapable of assuming this inferior role for very long and, in the vicinity of the twentieth year, generally prefers to abandon man to his lusterless fate.

Though he may later try to pull himself together upon occasion, having felt that he is losing by slow degrees all reason for living, incapable as he has become of being able to rise to some exceptional situation such as love, he will hardly succeed. This is because he henceforth belongs body and soul to an imperative practical necessity which demands his constant attention. None of his gestures will be expansive, none of his ideas generous or far-reaching. In his mind's eye, events real or imagined will be seen only as they relate to a welter of similar events, events in which he has not participated, *abortive* events. What am I saying: he will judge them in relationship to one of these events whose consequences are more reassuring than the others. On no account will he view them as his salvation.

Beloved imagination, what I most like in you is your unsparing quality.

The mere word "freedom" is the only one that still excites me. I deem it capable of indefinitely sustaining the old human fanaticism. It doubtless satisfies my only legitimate aspiration. Among all the many misfortunes to which we are heir, it is only fair to admit that we are allowed the greatest degree of freedom of thought. It is up to us not to misuse it. To reduce the imagination to a state of slavery—even though it would mean the elimination of what is commonly called happiness—is to betray all sense of absolute justice within oneself. Imagination alone offers me some intimation of what *can be,* and this is enough to remove to some slight degree the terrible injunction;

enough, too, to allow me to devote myself to it without fear of making a mistake (as though it were possible to make a bigger mistake). Where does it begin to turn bad, and where does the mind's stability cease? For the mind, is the possibility of erring not rather the contingency of good?

There remains madness, "the madness that one locks up," as it has aptly been described. That madness or another.... We all know, in fact, that the insane owe their incarceration to a tiny number of legally reprehensible acts and that, were it not for these acts, their freedom (or what we see as their freedom) would not be threatened. I am willing to admit that they are, to some degree, victims of their imagination, in that it induces them not to pay attention to certain rules—outside of which the species feels itself threatened—which we are all supposed to know and respect. But their profound indifference to the way in which we judge them, and even to the various punishments meted out to them, allows us to suppose that they derive a great deal of comfort and consolation from their imagination, that they enjoy their madness sufficiently to endure the thought that its validity does not extend beyond themselves. And, indeed, hallucinations, illusions, etc., are not a source of trifling pleasure. The best controlled sensuality partakes of it, and I know that there are many evenings when I would gladly tame that pretty hand which, during the last pages of Taine's *L'Intelligence,* indulges in some curious misdeeds. I could spend my whole life prying loose the secrets of the insane. These people are honest to a fault, and their naiveté has no peer but my own. Christopher Columbus should have set out to discover America with a boatload of madmen. And note how this madness has taken shape, and endured. [...]

We are still living under the reign of logic: this, of course, is what I have been driving at. But in this day and age logical methods are applicable only to solving problems of secondary interest. The absolute rationalism that is still in vogue allows us to consider only facts relating directly to our experience. Logical ends, on the contrary, escape us. It is pointless to add that experience itself has found itself increasingly circumscribed. It paces back and forth in a cage from which it is more and more difficult to make it emerge. It too leans for support on what is most immediately expedient, and it is protected by the sentinels of common sense. Under the pretense of civilization and progress, we have managed to banish from the mind everything that may rightly or wrongly be termed superstition, or fancy; forbidden is any kind of search for truth which is not in conformance with accepted practices. It was, apparently, by pure chance that a part of our mental world which we pretended not to be concerned with any longer—and, in my opinion by far the most important part—has been brought back to light. For this we must give thanks to the discoveries of Sigmund Freud. On the basis of these discoveries a current of opinion is finally forming by means of which the human explorer will be able to carry his investigations much further, authorized as he will henceforth be not to confine himself solely to the most summary realities. The imagination is perhaps on the point of reasserting itself, of reclaiming its rights. If the depths of our mind contain within it strange forces capable of augmenting those on the surface, or of waging a victorious battle against them, there is every reason to seize them—first to seize them, then, if need be, to submit them to the control of our reason. The analysts themselves have everything to gain by it. But it is worth noting that no means has been designated a priori for carrying out this undertaking, that until further notice it can be construed to be the province of poets as well as scholars, and that its success is not dependent upon the more or less capricious paths that will be followed.

Freud very rightly brought his critical faculties to bear upon the dream. It is, in fact, inadmissible that this considerable portion of psychic activity (since, at least from man's birth until his death, thought offers no solution of continuity, the sum of the moments of dream, from the point of view of time, and taking into consideration only the time of pure dreaming, that is the dreams of sleep, is not inferior to the sum of the moments of reality, or, to be more precisely limiting, the moments of waking) has still today been so grossly neglected. I have always been amazed at the way an ordinary observer lends so much more credence and attaches so much more importance to waking events than to those occurring in dreams. It is because man, when he ceases to sleep, is above all the plaything of his memory, and in its normal state memory takes pleasure in weakly retracing for him the circumstances of the dream, in stripping it of any real importance, and in dismissing the only *determinant* from the point where he thinks he has left it a few hours before: this firm hope, this concern. He is under the impression of continuing something that is worthwhile. Thus the dream finds itself reduced to a mere parenthesis, as is the night. And, like the night, dreams generally contribute little to furthering our understanding. This curious state of affairs seems to me to call for certain reflections:

1) Within the limits where they operate (or are thought to operate) dreams give every evidence of being continuous and show signs of organization. Memory alone arrogates to itself the right to excerpt from dreams, to ignore the transitions, and to depict for us rather a series of dreams than the *dream itself*. By the same token, at any given moment we have only a distinct notion of realities, the coordination of which is a question of will.* What is worth

---

*Account must be taken of the *depth* of the dream. For the most part I retain only what I can glean from its most superficial layers. What I most enjoy contemplating about a dream is everything that sinks back below the surface in a waking state, everything I have forgotten about my activities in the course of the preceding day, dark foliage, stupid branches. In "reality," likewise, I prefer to *fall*.

noting is that nothing allows us to presuppose a greater dissipation of the elements of which the dream is constituted. I am sorry to have to speak about it according to a formula which in principle excludes the dream. When will we have sleeping logicians, sleeping philosophers? I would like to sleep, in order to surrender myself to the dreamers, the way I surrender myself to those who read me with eyes wide open; in order to stop imposing, in this realm, the conscious rhythm of my thought. Perhaps my dream last night follows that of the night before, and will be continued the next night, with an exemplary strictness. *It's quite possible,* as the saying goes. And since it has not been proved in the slightest that, in doing so, the "reality" with which I am kept busy continues to exist in the state of dream, that it does not sink back down into the immemorial, why should I not grant to dreams what I occasionally refuse reality, that is, this value of certainty in itself which, in its own time, is not open to my repudiation? Why should I not expect from the sign of the dream more than I expect from a degree of consciousness which is daily more acute? Can't the dream also be used in solving the fundamental questions of life? Are these questions the same in one case as in the other and, in the dream, do these questions already exist? Is the dream any less restrictive or punitive than the rest? I am growing old and, more than that reality to which I believe I subject myself, it is perhaps the dream, the difference with which I treat the dream, which makes me grow old.

2) Let me come back again to the waking state. I have no choice but to consider it a phenomenon of interference. Not only does the mind display, in this state, a strange tendency to lose its bearings (as evidenced by the slips and mistakes the secrets of which are just beginning to be revealed to us), but, what is more, it

does not appear that, when the mind is functioning normally, it really responds to anything but the suggestions which come to it from the depths of that dark night to which I commend it. However conditioned it may be, its balance is relative. It scarcely dares express itself and, if it does, it confines itself to verifying that such and such an idea, or such and such a woman, has made an impression on it. What impression it would be hard pressed to say, by which it reveals the degree of its subjectivity, and nothing more. This idea, this woman, disturb it, they tend to make it less severe. What they do is isolate the mind for a second from its solvent and spirit it to heaven, as the beautiful precipitate it can be, that it is. When all else fails, it then calls upon chance, a divinity even more obscure than the others to whom it ascribes all its aberrations. Who can say to me that the angle by which that idea which affects it is offered, that what it likes in the eye of that woman is not precisely what links it to its dream, binds it to those fundamental facts which, through its own fault, it has lost? And if things were different, what might it be capable of? I would like to provide it with the key to this corridor.

3) The mind of the man who dreams is fully satisfied by what happens to him. The agonizing question of possibility is no longer pertinent. Kill, fly faster, love to your heart's content. And if you should die, are you not certain of reawaking among the dead? Let yourself be carried along, events will not tolerate your interference. You are nameless. The ease of everything is priceless.

What reason, I ask, a reason so much vaster than the other, makes dreams seem so natural and allows me to welcome unreservedly a welter of episodes so strange that they would confound me now as I write? And yet I can believe my eyes, my ears; this great day has arrived, this beast has spoken.

If man's awaking is harder, if it breaks the spell too abruptly, it is because he has been led to make for himself too impoverished a notion of atonement.

4) From the moment when it is subjected to a methodical examination, when, by means yet to be determined, we succeed in recording the contents of dreams in their entirety (and that presupposes a discipline of memory spanning generations; but let us nonetheless begin by noting the most salient facts), when its graph will expand with unparalleled volume and regularity, we may hope that the mysteries which really are not will give way to the great Mystery. I believe in the future resolution of these two states, dream and reality, which are seemingly so contradictory, into a kind of absolute reality, a *surreality,* if one may so speak. It is in quest of this surreality that I am going, certain not to find it but too unmindful of my death not to calculate to some slight degree the joys of its possession.

A story is told according to which Saint-Pol-Roux, in times gone by, used to have a notice posted on the door of his manor house in Camaret, every evening before he went to sleep, which read: THE POET IS WORKING.

A great deal more could be said, but in passing I merely wanted to touch upon a subject which in itself would require a very long and much more detailed discussion; I shall come back to it. At this juncture, my intention was merely to mark a point by noting the *hate of the marvelous* which rages in certain men, this absurdity beneath which they try to bury it. Let us not mince words: the marvelous is always beautiful, anything marvelous is beautiful, in fact only the marvelous is beautiful. […]

1924 · RS & HRL

BURIAL DENIED

If it was already behind the times to speak of Anatole France while he was alive, let's at least give a grateful nod to the newspaper that's carrying him off, the wicked daily that had brought him forth. Loti, Barrès, France. All things considered, let's mark in beautiful white the year that put down those three sinister clowns: the idiot, the traitor, and the cop. We should—no objections from me—reserve a special word of scorn for the latter. With France, we're losing a bit of human servility. They should declare a national holiday to commemorate the end of his craftiness, traditionalism, patriotism, opportunism, skepticism, realism, and coldness! Let's not forget that the vilest hypocrites of our time claimed Anatole France as an accomplice and let's never forgive him for having draped his smiling inertia in the colors of the Revolution. To bury his corpse, someone ought to dump the old books "he loved so well" from one of those stalls along the quays, stuff him inside, and toss the whole thing into the Seine. Now that he's dead, the man mustn't be allowed to shed any more dust.

FROM *A CORPSE*; OCTOBER 1924 • MP

from SECOND MANIFESTO
OF SURREALISM

In spite of the various efforts peculiar to each of those who used to claim kinship with Surrealism, or who still do, one must ultimately admit that, more than anything else, Surrealism attempted to provoke, from the intellectual and moral point of view, *an attack of conscience,* of the most general and serious kind, and that the extent to which this was or was not accomplished alone can determine its historical success or failure.

From the intellectual point of view, it was then, and still is today, a question of testing by any and all means, and of demonstrating at any price, the meretricious nature of the old antinomies hypocritically intended to prevent any unusual ferment on the part of man, were it only by giving him a vague idea of the means at his disposal, by challenging him to escape to some meaningful degree from the universal fetters. The bugaboo of death, the simplistic theatrical portrayal of the beyond, the shipwreck of the most beautiful reason in sleep, the overwhelming curtain of the future, the tower of Babel, the mirrors of inconstancy, the impassable silver wall bespattered with brains—these all too gripping images of the human catastrophe are, perhaps, no more than images. Everything tends to make us believe that there exists a certain point of the mind at which life and death, the real and the imagined, past and future, the communicable and the incommunicable, high and low, cease to be perceived as contradictions. Now search as one may one will never find any other motivating force in the activities of the Surrealists than the hope of finding and fixing this point. From this it becomes obvious how absurd it would be to define Surrealism solely as constructive or destructive: the point to which we are referring is a fortiori that point where construction and destruction can no longer be brandished one against the other. It is also clear that Surrealism is not interested in giving very serious consideration to anything that happens outside of itself, under the guise of art, or even anti-art, of philosophy or anti-philosophy—in short, of anything not aimed at the annihilation of the being into a diamond, all blind and interior, which is no more the soul of ice than that of fire. What could those people who are still concerned about the position they occupy *in the world* expect from the Surrealist experiment? In this mental site, from which one can no longer set forth except for oneself on a dangerous but, we think, supreme feat of reconnaissance, it is likewise out of the question that the slightest heed be paid to the footsteps of those who arrive or to the footsteps of those who leave, since these footsteps occur in a region where by definition Surrealism has no ear to hear. We would not want Surrealism to be at the mercy of the whims of this or that group of persons; if it declares that it is able, by its own means, to uproot thought from an increasingly cruel state of thralldom, to steer it back onto the path of total comprehension, return it to its original purity—that is enough for it to be judged only on what it has done and what it still has to do in order to keep its promises.

Before proceeding, however, to verify the balance sheet, it is worthwhile to know just what kind of moral virtues Surrealism lays claim to, since, moreover, it plunges its roots into life and, no doubt not by chance, into *the life of this period,* seeing that I laden this life with anecdotes like the sky, the sound of a watch, the cold, a malaise, that is, I begin to speak about it in a vulgar manner. To think these things, to hold any rung whatever of this weather-beaten ladder—none of us is beyond such things until he has passed through the last stage of asceticism. It is in fact from the disgusting cauldron of these meaningless mental images that the desire to proceed beyond the insufficient, the absurd, distinction between the beautiful and the ugly, true and false, good and evil, is born and sustained. And, as it is the degree of resistance that this choice idea meets with which determines the more or less certain flight of the mind toward a world at last inhabitable, one can understand why Surrealism was not afraid to make for itself a tenet of total revolt, complete insubordination, of sabotage according to rule, and why it still expects nothing save from violence. The simplest Surrealist act consists of dashing down into the street, pistol in hand, and firing blindly, as fast as you can pull the trigger, into the crowd. Anyone who, at least once in his life, has not dreamed of thus putting an end to the petty system of debasement and cretinization in effect has a well-defined place in that crowd, with his belly at barrel level.* The justification of such an act is, to my mind, in no way in-

*I know that these last two sentences are going to delight a certain number of simpletons who have been trying for a long time to catch me up in a contradiction with myself. Thus, am I really saying that "the simplest Surrealist act ..."? So what if I am! And while some, with an obvious axe to grind, seize the opportunity to ask me "what I'm waiting for," others raise a hue and cry about anarchy and try to pretend that they have caught me in *flagrante delicto* committing an act of revolutionary indiscipline. Nothing is easier for me than to deprive these people of the cheap effect they might have. Yes, I am concerned to learn whether a person is blessed with violence before asking myself whether, in that person, violence *compromises* or *does not compromise.* I believe in the absolute virtue of anything that takes place, spontaneously or not, in the sense of nonacceptance, and no reasons of general efficacity,

compatible with the belief in that gleam of light that Surrealism seeks to detect deep within us. I simply wanted to bring in here the element of human despair, on this side of which nothing would be able to justify that belief. It is impossible to give one's assent to one and not to the other. Anyone who should pretend to embrace this belief without truly sharing this despair would soon be revealed as an enemy. This frame of mind which we call Surrealist and which we see thus occupied with itself, seems less and less to require any historical antecedents and, so far as I am personally concerned, I have no objection if reporters, judicial experts, and others hold it to be specifically modern. I have more confidence in this moment, this present moment, of my thought than in the sum total of everything people may try to read into a finished work, into a human life that has reached the end of its road. There is nothing more sterile, in the final analysis, than that perpetual interrogation of the dead: did Rimbaud become converted on the eve of his death? can one find in Lenin's last will and testament sufficient evidence to condemn the present policy of the Third International? was an unbearable, and completely personal, disgrace the mainspring of Alphonse Rabbe's pessimism? did Sade, in plenary session of the National Convention, commit a counterrevolutionary act?

from which long, prerevolutionary patience draws its inspiration—reasons to which I defer—will make me deaf to the cry which can be wrenched from us at every moment by the frightful disproportion between what is gained and what is lost, between what is granted and what is suffered. As for that act that I term the simplest: it is clear that my intention is not to recommend it above every other because it is simple, and to try and pick a quarrel with me on this point is tantamount to asking, in bourgeois fashion, any nonconformist why he doesn't commit suicide, or any revolutionary why he doesn't pack up and go live in the U.S.S.R. Don't come to me with such stories! The haste with which certain people would be only too happy to see me disappear, coupled with my own natural tendency to agitation, are in themselves sufficient reason for me not to clear out of here for no good reason.

It is enough to allow these questions to be asked to appreciate the fragility of the evidence of those who are no longer among us. Too many rogues and rascals are interested in the success of this undertaking of spiritual highway robbery for me to follow them over this terrain. When it comes to revolt, none of us must have any need of ancestors. I would like to make it very clear that in my opinion it is necessary to hold the cult of men in deep distrust, however great they may seemingly be. With one exception—Lautréamont—I do not see a single one of them who has not left some questionable trace in his wake. Useless to cite the example of Rimbaud again: Rimbaud was mistaken, Rimbaud wanted to fool us. He is guilty in our eyes for having allowed, for not having made completely impossible, certain disparaging interpretations of his thought, such as those made by Paul Claudel. So much the worse for Baudelaire too ("O Satan . . .") and that "eternal rule" of his life: "to say a prayer every morning to God, *source of all strength and all justice, to my father, to Mariette, and to Poe,* as intercessors." The right to contradict himself, I know, but really! To God, to Poe? Poe who, in the police magazines, is today so properly presented as the *master of scientific policemen* (from Sherlock Holmes, in fact, to Paul Valéry . . .). Is it not a shame to present in an intellectually attractive light a type of policeman, *always a policeman,* to bestow upon the world a police *method?* Let us, in passing, spit on Edgar Poe.* If, through Surrealism, we reject unhesitatingly the notion of

*At the time of the original publication of *Marie Roget,* footnotes at the bottom of the pages were considered superfluous. But several years have passed since the event on which this story is based occurred, and it seemed worthwhile to us to restore them here, together with a few words of explanation relative to the general scheme of things. A girl, Mary Cecilia Rogers, was murdered in the vicinity of New York; and although her death aroused a strong and continuing interest, the mystery surrounding her death was still not solved at the time this piece was written and published (November 1842). Here, under the pretext of relating the fate of a Parisian

the sole possibility of the things which "are," and if we ourselves de-
clare that by a path which "is," a path which we can show and help
people to follow, one can arrive at what people claimed "was not," if
we cannot find words enough to stigmatize the baseness of Western
thought, if we are not afraid to take up arms against logic, if we refuse
to swear that something we do in dreams is less meaningful than
something we do in a state of waking, if we are not even sure that we
will not do away *with time,* that sinister old farce, that train constantly
jumping off the track, mad pulsation, inextricable conglomeration of
breaking and broken beasts, how do you expect us to show any ten-
derness, even to be tolerant, toward an apparatus of social conserva-
tion, of whatever sort it may be? That would be the only madness
truly unacceptable on our part. Everything remains to be done, every
means must be worth trying, in order to lay waste to the ideas of *fam-
ily, country, religion.* No matter how well known the Surrealist posi-
tion may be with respect to this matter, still it must be stressed that on
this point there is no room for compromise. [...]

But he loved Paris.

girl of easy virtue, the author scrupulously traced the essential facts, and at the same
time gave the nonessential and simply parallel facts of the actual murder of Mary
Rogers. Thus any argument founded on fiction is applicable to the truth; and the
search for the truth is the goal.

"*The Mystery of Marie Roget* was composed far from the theater of the crime, and
without any other means of investigation save the newspapers the author was able
to procure for himself. Thus he had to do without a great number of documents he
could have used to good advantage if he had been in the country and if he had in-
spected the localities. It is worthwhile pointing out, nonetheless, that the confes-
sions of two persons (one of whom is the Madame Deluc of the novel), made at
different times and long after the publication of this work, fully confirmed not only
the general conclusion but also *all* the principal hypothetical details on which this
conclusion had been based." (Introductory note to *The Mystery of Marie Roget.*)

1929 · RS & HRL

SIMULATION OF GENERAL
PARALYSIS ESSAYED

Thou my great one whom I adore beautiful as the whole earth and in the most beautiful stars of the earth that I adore thou my great woman adored by all the powers of the stars beautiful with the beauty of the thousands of millions of queens who adorn the earth the adoration that I have for thy beauty brings me to my knees to beg thee to think of me I am brought to my knees I adore thy beauty think of me thou my adorable beauty my great beauty whom I adore I roll the diamonds in the moss loftier than the forest whose most lofty hair of thine think of me—forget me not my little woman when possible at ingle-nook on the sand of emerald—look at thyself in my hand that keeps me steadfast on the whole world so that thou mayest recognize me for what I am my dark-fair woman my beautiful one my foolish one think of me in paradises my head in my hands.

They were not enough for me the hundred and twenty castles where we were going to love one another to-morrow they shall build me a hundred thousand more I have hunted forests of baobabs from thine eyes peacocks panthers and lyre-birds I will shut them up in my strongholds and we will go and walk together in the forests of Asia Europe Africa America that surround our castles in the admirable forests of thine eyes that are used to my splendour.

Thou hast not to wait for the surprise that I want to give thee for thine anniversary that falls to-day the same day as mine—I give it to thee at once since I have waited fifteen times for the year one thousand before giving thee the surprise of asking thee to think of me in hide-and-seek—I want thee laughing to think of me my young eternal woman. Before falling to sleep I have counted clouds and clouds of chariots full of beets for the sun and I want to bring thee to the astrakan shore that is being built on two horizons for thine eyes of petrol to wage war I will lead thee by paths of diamonds paved with primroses with emeralds and the cloak of ermine that I want to cover thee with is a bird of prey the diamonds that thy feet shall tread I got them cut in the shape of a butterfly.

Think of me whose only thought is the glory wherein the dazzling wealth of an earth and all the skies that I have conquered for thee slumber I adore thee and I adore thine eyes and I have opened thine eyes open to all those whom they have seen and I will give to all the beings whom thine eyes have seen raiment of gold and crystal raiment that they must cast away when thine eyes have tarnished them with their disdain. I bleed in my heart at the very initials of thy name that are all the letters beginning with z in the infinity of alphabets and civilizations where I will love thee still since thou art willing to be my woman and to think of me in the countries where there is no mean.

My heart bleeds on thy mouth and closes on thy mouth on all the red chestnut-trees of the avenue of thy mouth where we are on our way through the shining dust to lie us down amidst the meteors of thy beauty that I adore my great one who art so beautiful that I am happy to adorn my treasures with thy presence with thy thought and with thy name that multiplies the facets of the ecstasy of my treasures with thy name that I adore because it wakes an echo in all the mirrors of beauty of my splendour my original woman my scaffolding of rosewood thou art the fault of my fault of my very great fault as Jesus Christ is the woman of my cross—twelve times twelve thousand one hundred and forty-nine times I have loved thee with passion on the way and I am crucified to north east west and north for thy kiss of radium and I want thee and in my mirror of pearls thou art the breath of him who shall not rise again to the surface and who loves thee in adoration my woman lying upright when thou art seated combing thyself.

Thou art coming thou thinkest of me thou art coming on thy thirteen full legs and on all thine empty legs that beat the air with the swaying of thine arms a multitude of arms that want to clasp me kneeling between thy legs and thine arms to clasp me without fear lest my locomotives should prevent thee from coming to me and I am thou and I am before thee to stop thee to give thee all the stars of the sky in one kiss on thine eyes all the kisses of the world in one star on thy mouth.

Thine in flames.

PS.—I would like a Street Directory for mass a Street Directory with a knotted cord to mark the place. Bring also a Franco-German flag that I may plant it in No Man's Land. And a pound of that chocolate with the little girl who sticks the placards (I forget). And then again nine of those little girls with their lawyers and their judges and come in the special train with the speed of light and the outlaws of the Far West to distract me for a moment who am popping here unfortunately like champagne corks. The left strap of my braces has just broken I was lifting the world as though it were a feather. Canst thou do something for me buy a tank I want to see thee coming like fairies.

WITH PAUL ELUARD; 1930 · SB

from THE AUTOMATIC MESSAGE

[…] The history of automatic writing in Surrealism—and I'm not afraid to say it—is one of continual misfortune. Indeed, not even the underhanded protests of the critics, who have been particularly attentive and hostile on this point, will keep me from recognizing that, for years, I counted on the torrential outpouring of automatic writing to cleanse the literary stables once and for all. In this regard, the desire to throw open the floodgates will certainly remain the generative idea of Surrealism. It says something that, in my eyes, the movement's partisans and adversaries will always and easily be defined by whether they value only the authenticity of the automatic product or whether, on the contrary, they wish to see it reconciled with something other than itself. Quality, here as elsewhere, could not help becoming a function of quantity. If there was no lack of quantity, some easily imagined factors kept it from acting on the public scale as a force of submersion: thousands of notebooks, *each as good as the next,* have remained in desk drawers. The important thing, moreover, is for more such notebooks to be filled, an infinite number—and better still, for their authors frequently to compare their method with ours and to admit to us openly their technical concerns.

Although I never sought to codify the ways in which this highly personal and infinitely variable dictation was obtained, I have not been able to avoid (by suggesting certain modes of behavior) simplifying the *listening* conditions to an extreme degree, nor generalizing totally individual methods of resumption in case the current was interrupted. I also omitted, even in a series of publications that came after the first *Manifesto,* to specify the nature of the obstacles that often conspire to divert the verbal outflow from its original direction. Whence the very legitimate questions—which furthermore did not meet the slightest objection—that I have sometimes been asked: How can one ensure the homogeneity or remedy the heterogeneity of the constituent parts of such a discourse, which often seems to contain scraps of several discourses? What should one make of interference or gaps? How can one keep from visualizing up to a certain point what is being said? How can one tolerate the distressing passage from the auditory to the visual? etc. It is unfortunately quite true that up until now, those who dipped "poetically" into automatic writing have not all been equally concerned with such questions. Many, in fact, have preferred to see automatic writing only as a new science of literary *effects,* which they blithely adapted to the needs of their little industry. I believe I can say that the automatic flux, which they had flattered themselves they could use at their leisure, lost no time in abandoning them completely. Others spontaneously contented themselves with a half-measure that consists in encouraging the eruption of automatic language in the midst of more or less conscious developments. Finally, we must note that numerous pastiches of automatic texts have recently been put into circulation—texts that are not always easy to distinguish at first glance from authentic examples, because we lack objective, original criteria. These obscurities, these failings, these stagnations, these efforts at simulation seem to demand more imperiously than ever, for the benefit of the actions we mean to carry out, a complete *return to first principles.* […]

Surrealism's distinctive feature is to have proclaimed the total equality of all normal human beings before the subliminal message, to have constantly maintained that this message constitutes a common patrimony, of which everyone is entitled to a share, and which must very soon, and at all costs, stop being seen as the prerogative of the chosen few. I say that every man and every woman deserves to be convinced of their ability to tap into this language at will, which has nothing supernatural about it and which, for each and every one of us, is *the* vehicle of revelation. In order to do this, it is crucial that they revise their narrow and erroneous conception of such specific vocations, whether artistic or mediumistic. If one looked closely, one would in fact discover that every vocation has originated in a fortuitous accident, whose effect has been to undermine certain resistances in the individual. For whoever is concerned with something other than his prosaic, immediate interest, the essential thing is that these resistances can be undermined. […] Automatic writing—which is easy and attractive, and which we hoped to put within *everyone's* reach by eliminating the unnerving and cumbersome apparatus of hypnosis—seems, regardless of such obstacles, to be what Schrenck-Notzing wanted to see it as, namely, "a sure means of favoring the outpouring of psychic faculties, and particularly artistic talents, by focusing one's consciousness on the task at hand and by freeing the individual from the inhibitory factors that restrain and trouble him, sometimes utterly blocking the exercise of his latent gifts."

This standpoint of artistic talent, and the incredible vanity that goes along with it, is naturally a large part of the internal and external causes of distrust that, in Surrealism, have prevented automatic writing from fulfilling all its promises. Although the original aim was simply to seize involuntary verbal representations in their continuity and fix them in writing, while avoiding any qualitative judgments, critical comparisons could not avoid showing that the internal language of different writers displayed unequal levels of richness and elegance—which was fertile terrain for despicable poetic rivalries. In most cases, furthermore, an inevitable, subsequent delight in the very terms of the texts obtained, and specifically in the images and symbolic figures with which they abounded, also helped undermine the indifference and distraction that these authors needed to maintain toward their texts (at least while producing them). [...] Now, if automatic dictation can be obtained with a certain continuity, the process by which these images develop and join together is very difficult to grasp. As far as we can tell, their nature is eruptive. So it was that on the very evening (September 27) that I noted the two sentences at the beginning of this article, just when I had given up in my subsequent attempts to provoke a verbal equivalent, I suddenly saw myself (my hand?) rolling the edges—as one does to prepare a paper filter—or reducing the sides of a kind of scallop shell. Without a doubt, I took this as another form of automatism. Was it obtained in compensation for the verbal one that I was trying too hard to hear? I don't know. Nonetheless (and this is the main thing), I consider verbal inspirations infinitely richer in visual meaning, infinitely more resistant to the eye, than visual images properly speaking. Whence my constant protest against the poet's so-called "visionary" power. No, Lautréamont and Rimbaud did not *see,* did not experience *a priori* what they described; which is tantamount to saying that they didn't describe it at all, but rather that they limited themselves in the dark corridors of their being to listening—indistinctly and, while they wrote, without understanding them any more than we do when we first read them—to certain accomplished and accomplishable works. "Illumination" comes *afterward.* [...]

19 FEBRUARY 1896 André Breton is born in Tinchebray (Normandy), France, and spends his early childhood in Brittany. His father is an ex-policeman and small businessman, his mother a seamstress. In the 1930s, for personal and astrological reasons, Breton will change his birthdate to February 18, the date most commonly reproduced in summaries of his life.

1900–1914 The Bretons live in the Paris suburbs, where Breton attends school, composes Symbolist-inspired poetry, and begins studying medicine.

1915 Breton is drafted into the army as a medical orderly; he discovers Freud's theories and treats psychiatric patients, which profoundly shapes his ideas about the mind and the unconscious. Soon afterward, he meets the enigmatic dandy Jacques Vaché, who inspires a radical reexamination of his views about literature and art.

1919 Following Vaché's mysterious death, Breton composes the automatic text *The Magnetic Fields* with Philippe Soupault and becomes interested in the flamboyantly nihilistic Dada movement. When Dada's leader, Tristan Tzara, comes to Paris the following year, Breton throws himself into the movement's frenzied activities. *Pawnshop,* Breton's first book of poems, is published.

1921–1923 Breton marries Simone Kahn and moves into a studio at 42 Rue Fontaine, his address for the rest of his life. His second book of poems, *Earthlight,* is published in 1923.

1924 Having broken with Dada, Breton launches the Surrealist movement and publishes *Manifesto of Surrealism.* The movement, initially defined by its interest in dreams and automatism, counts some of the century's most original minds as its early members: Louis Aragon and Paul Eluard (Breton's closest friends), Robert Desnos, Max Ernst, Antonin Artaud, Jacques Prévert, Yves Tanguy, Benjamin Péret, Raymond Queneau, Michel Leiris, André Masson, and Man Ray.

1926 Breton meets Nadja, who inspires his best-known work. That same year, seeking to have an impact on social and political mores, he begins a tumultuous association with the Communists and briefly joins the Party in 1927.

1929 By this time, Breton's political convictions have led to the exclusion of numerous Surrealists from the movement and to the inflammatory *Second Manifesto of Surrealism*. Several of those excluded respond with the violently anti-Breton pamphlet *A Corpse* (reprising the title of an earlier Surrealist pamphlet). That same year, Breton divorces Simone. Salvador Dalí, Luis Buñuel, René Char, and Alberto Giacometti join Surrealism.

1932 Despite Breton's overtures, the Communist Party (now heavily Stalinist) remains skeptical about Surrealism. Breton's relations with the Party are further strained that spring, when Aragon leaves Surrealism to become a Communist. Breton's third collection, *The White-Haired Revolver*, recapitulates all of his poetry up to that time.

1934 Breton meets and marries Jacqueline Lamba, who inspires his book *Mad Love*, and with whom he has a daughter.

1935 Breton finally breaks with the Communist Party, after being denied permission to speak at the Congress of Writers for the Defense of Culture. Although he will remain politically active for the rest of his life, from this moment on he is an outspoken opponent of Stalinism, and he will be among the first in France to denounce the infamous Moscow Trials.

1938 A major retrospective of Surrealist art is held in February. Breton, a long-standing admirer of Leon Trotsky, visits the exiled revolutionary in Mexico and drafts with him the "Manifesto for an Independent Revolutionary Art" (co-signed by Diego Rivera for security reasons). On his return to France, he helps found the Trotskyist association F.I.A.R.I. But the war aborts this project, and after the French defeat, Breton, fearing Vichy repression, leaves Europe with his family.

1941–1946 Breton takes refuge in New York, where he organizes various Surrealist activities with fellow exiles Masson, Ernst, Claude Lévi-Strauss, and Marcel Duchamp. During this period, he divorces Jacqueline and marries Elisa Claro.

1946–1948 Breton and Elisa return to France. He stages an ambitious Surrealist art exhibition and tries to renew contact with his former colleagues, but many have conflicting allegiances (particularly to Stalinism, as in the case of Aragon and Eluard), and by the early 1950s few of the prewar Surrealists are left in the group. He publishes his last important collection of verse, *Poèmes*, which contains work from the early years through his most recent poems.

1951 The "Carrouges Affair," which alienates many remaining Surrealists, further isolates Breton from his generation.

1952 Broadcast and publication of Breton's *Conversations* with André Parinaud, which introduces Surrealism to a mainstream audience.

1952–1953 Brief collaboration between the Surrealists and the anarchists. Publication of the essay collection *Free Rein,* Breton's last major book.

1950s–1960s Flanked by an ever-growing circle of younger men and women, Breton continues to lead Surrealism as an organized movement until his death on 28 September 1966.

ACKNOWLEDGMENTS

Unless otherwise indicated, all works cited are by André Breton.

POEMS

"Merry" (Rieuse) was first published in *Mont de Piété* (1919). Reprinted by permission of Editions Gallimard, Paris. This translation first appeared in *Conversations: The Autobiography of Surrealism,* trans. Mark Polizzotti (New York: Paragon House, 1993). Reprinted by permission.

"Way" (Façon), "Age" (Age), "Black Forest" (Forêt noire), and "Mister V" (Monsieur V) were first published in *Mont de Piété.* These translations first appeared in *Earthlight,* trans. Bill Zavatsky and Zack Rogow (Los Angeles: Sun & Moon Press, 1993). English translation copyright © 1985, 1986, 1991, 1993 by Bill Zavatsky and Zack Rogow. Reprinted by permission of Sun & Moon Press.

"For Lafcadio" (Pour Lafcadio) and "The Mystery Corset" (Le Corset mystère) were first published in *Mont de Piété.* Reprinted by permission of Editions Gallimard, Paris. These translations are previously unpublished.

The Magnetic Fields (Les Champs magnétiques) by André Breton and Philippe Soupault was first published in 1920. Reprinted by permission of Editions Gallimard, Paris. This translation first appeared in *The Magnetic Fields,* trans. David Gascoyne (London: Atlas Press, 1985). Reprinted by permission.

"Counterfeit Coin" (Pièce fausse), "PSST" (PSTT), "In the Eyes of the Gods" (Au regard des divinités), and "Choose Life" (Plutôt la vie) were first published in *Clair de terre* (1923). These translations first appeared in *Earthlight.* Reprinted by permission of Sun & Moon Press.

"No Way Out of Here" (Il n'y a pas à sortir de là) and "Sunflower" (Tournesol) were first published in *Clair de terre*. Reprinted by permission of Editions Gallimard, Paris. These translations are previously unpublished.

"Angle of Sight" (L'Angle de mire) was first published, untitled, in *Manifeste du surréalisme* (1924) and then in *Le Revolver aux cheveux blancs* (1932). Reprinted by permission of Editions Gallimard, Paris. This translation is previously unpublished.

"Soluble Fish" (Poisson soluble) was first published in *Manifeste du surréalisme*. This translation is from *Manifestoes of Surrealism,* trans. Richard Seaver and Helen R. Lane (Ann Arbor: University of Michigan Press, 1969). Reprinted by permission of University of Michigan Press.

"Make it so daylight . . ." (Fais que le jour) was not published in Breton's lifetime. This translation first appeared in *My Heart Through Which Her Heart Has Passed: Poems of Love and Desperation,* trans. Mark Polizzotti (Paris and London: Alyscamps Press, 1998). Reprinted by permission.

"I Listen to Myself Still Talking" (Je m'écoute encore parler) was first published in *Ralentir travaux* by André Breton, Paul Eluard, and René Char (1930). Reprinted by permission of Editions Gallimard, Paris. This translation first appeared in *Ralentir Travaux,* trans. Keith Waldrop (Cambridge, Mass.: Exact Change, 1990). Reprinted by permission of Keith Waldrop.

"The Writings Depart" (Les Ecrits s'en vont), "The Forest in the Axe" (La Forêt dans la hache), "Curtain Curtain" (Rideau rideau), and "Vigilance" (Vigilance) were first published in *Le Revolver aux cheveux blancs*. These translations first appeared in *Earthlight*. Reprinted by permission of Sun & Moon Press.

"No Grounds for Prosecution" (Non-lieu) was first published in *Le Revolver aux cheveux blancs*. This translation first appeared in *The Random House Book of Twentieth-Century French Poetry,* ed. Paul Auster (New York: Random House, 1982). Reprinted by permission of Paul Auster.

"After the Giant Anteater" (Après le grand tamanoir) was first published in *Le Revolver aux cheveux blancs*. This translation first appeared in *My Heart Through Which Her Heart Has Passed*. Reprinted by permission.

"Free Union" (L'Union libre) and "A Branch of Nettle Enters through the Window" (Une Branche d'ortie entre par la fenêtre) were first published in *Le Revolver aux cheveux blancs.* These translations are from *The Poetry of Surrealism,* ed. Michael Benedikt (Boston: Little, Brown and Co., 1974). Reprinted by permission of David Antin.

"Lethal Relief" (Le Grand Secours meurtrier) was first published in *Le Revolver aux cheveux blancs.* This translation first appeared in *This Quarter* (September 1932). Copyright © 1932 by Samuel Beckett. Reprinted by permission of Georges Borchardt, Inc., for the Estate of Samuel Beckett.

"In the lovely half-light of 1934 . . ." (Au beau demi-jour de 1934) was first published in *L'Air de l'eau* (1934). Reprinted by permission of Editions Gallimard, Paris. This translation is from *The Poetry of Surrealism.* Copyright © 1974 by Michael Benedikt. Reprinted by permission of Georges Borchardt, Inc., for Michael Benedikt.

"It was going on five in the morning . . ." (Il allait être cinq heures du matin) and "Always for the first time . . ." (Toujours pour la première fois) were first published in *L'Air de l'eau.* These translations first appeared in *Earthlight.* Reprinted by permission of Sun & Moon Press.

"Full Margin" (Pleine marge) was first published in *Poèmes* (1948). Reprinted by permission of Editions Gallimard, Paris. This translation is previously unpublished.

"Fata Morgana" first appeared in an English translation by Clark Mills in *New Directions* 41 (1941), and was first published in French in 1942 in *Les Lettres françaises* (Buenos Aires), before being reprinted in *Poèmes.* Reprinted by permission of Editions Gallimard, Paris. The current translation is previously unpublished.

"War" (Guerre) was first published in *Poèmes.* Reprinted by permission of Editions Gallimard, Paris. This translation is from *Young Cherry Trees Secured Against Hares,* trans. Edouard Roditi (Ann Arbor: University of Michigan Press, 1969). Reprinted by permission of Charles Henri Ford.

"Dreams" (Du rêve) was first published as part of the longer poem "Les Etats généraux" in *Poèmes.* Reprinted by permission of Editions Gallimard, Paris. This translation first appeared in *Translations by American Poets,* ed. Jean Garrigue (Athens: Ohio University Press, 1970). Reprinted with the permission of the Literary Estate of Robert Duncan. Copyright © the Literary Estate of Robert Duncan.

"Korwar" and "Rano Raraku" were first published as part of the poem cycle *Xénophiles,* in *Poèmes.* Reprinted by permission of Editions Gallimard, Paris. These translations first appeared in *Poems of André Breton: A Bilingual Anthology,* ed. and trans. Jean-Pierre Cauvin and Mary Ann Caws (Austin: University of Texas Press, 1982). Reprinted by permission of the translators.

"On the Road to San Romano" (Sur la route de San Romano) was first published in *Poèmes.* Reprinted by permission of Editions Gallimard, Paris. Version 1 first appeared in *The Poetry of Surrealism.* Copyright © 1974 by Michael Benedikt and Charles Simic. Reprinted by permission of Charles Simic and Georges Borchardt, Inc., for Michael Benedikt. Version 2 first appeared in *Ploughshares,* 11/4 (1986). Reprinted by permission of Richard Tillinghast.

Le La was first published in 1961. Reprinted by permission of Editions Gallimard, Paris. This translation is previously unpublished.

DOCUMENTS

"Subject" (Sujet) was first published in *Nord-Sud* 14 (April 1918). Reprinted by permission of Editions Gallimard, Paris. This translation is previously unpublished.

"The New Spirit" (L'Esprit nouveau) and "The Disdainful Confession" (La Confession dédaigneuse) were first published in *Les Pas perdus* (1924). These translations first appeared in *The Lost Steps,* trans. Mark Polizzotti (Lincoln: University of Nebraska Press, 1996). Reprinted by permission of University of Nebraska Press.

"Three Dreams" was first published in *La Révolution surréaliste* 1 (December 1924). This translation first appeared in *Sulfur* 45/46 (spring 2000). Reprinted by permission.

Manifesto of Surrealism (Manifeste du surréalisme) was first published in 1924. This translation first appeared in *Manifestoes of Surrealism,* trans. Richard Seaver and Helen R. Lane (Ann Arbor: University of Michigan Press, 1969). Reprinted by permission of University of Michigan Press.

"Burial Denied" (Défense d'inhumer) and "The Automatic Message" (Le Message automatique) were first published in *Point du jour* (1934). These translations first appeared in *Break of Day,* trans. Mark Polizzotti and Mary Ann Caws (Lincoln: University of Nebraska Press, 1999). Reprinted by permission of University of Nebraska Press.

Second Manifesto of Surrealism (Second manifeste du surréalisme) was first published in *La Révolution surréaliste* 12 (December 1929), and in book form in 1930.

This translation first appeared in *Manifestoes of Surrealism*. Reprinted by permission of University of Michigan Press.

"Simulation of General Paralysis Essayed" (Essai de paralysie générale) was published in *L'Immaculée conception* by André Breton and Paul Eluard (1930). Copyright © 1961 by Editions Pierre Seghers, Paris. This translation first appeared in *This Quarter* (September 1932). Copyright © 1932 by Samuel Beckett. Reprinted by permission of Georges Borchardt, Inc., for the Estate of Samuel Beckett.

SELECTED BIBLIOGRAPHY

WORKS OF ANDRÉ BRETON

Mont de Piété (1919).

Les Champs magnétiques [with Philippe Soupault] (1920). ENGLISH: *The Magnetic Fields,* trans. David Gascoyne. London: Atlas Press, 1985.

Clair de terre (1923).

Les Pas perdus (1924). ENGLISH: *The Lost Steps,* trans. Mark Polizzotti. Lincoln: University of Nebraska Press, 1996.

Manifeste du surréalisme (1924). ENGLISH (including *Soluble Fish, Second Manifesto of Surrealism,* and others): *Manifestoes of Surrealism,* trans. Richard Seaver and Helen R. Lane. Ann Arbor: University of Michigan Press, 1969.

Le Surréalisme et la peinture (1928; revised eds., 1946, 1965). ENGLISH: *Surrealism and Painting,* trans. Simon Watson Taylor. Boston: MFA Publications ("artWorks"), 2002.

Nadja (1928; revised ed., 1963). ENGLISH: *Nadja,* trans. Richard Howard. New York: Grove Press, 1960.

Ralentir travaux [with René Char and Paul Eluard] (1930). ENGLISH: *Ralentir Travaux,* trans. Keith Waldrop. Cambridge, Mass.: Exact Change, 1990.

Second Manifeste du surréalisme (1930).

L'Immaculée conception [with Paul Eluard] (1930). ENGLISH: *The Immaculate Conception,* trans. Jon Graham. London: Atlas Press, 1990.

Le Revolver aux cheveux blancs (1932).

Les Vases communicants (1932). ENGLISH: *Communicating Vessels,* trans. Mary Ann Caws and Geoffrey T. Harris. Lincoln: University of Nebraska Press, 1990.

Point du jour (1934). ENGLISH: *Break of Day,* trans. Mary Ann Caws and Mark Polizzotti. Lincoln: University of Nebraska Press, 1999.

L'Air de l'eau (1934).

L'Amour fou (1937). ENGLISH: *Mad Love,* trans. Mary Ann Caws. Lincoln: University of Nebraska Press, 1987.

Anthologie de l'humour noir ([1940]; revised eds., 1950, 1966). ENGLISH: *Anthology of Black Humor,* trans. Mark Polizzotti. San Francisco: City Lights Books, 1997.

Arcane 17 (1944; revised ed., 1947). ENGLISH: *Arcanum 17,* trans. Zack Rogow. Los Angeles: Sun & Moon Press, 1994.

Ode à Charles Fourier (1947). ENGLISH: *Ode to Charles Fourier,* trans. Kenneth White. New York: Grossman, 1970.

Martinique charmeuse de serpents [with André Masson] (1948).

Poèmes (1948).

Entretiens, 1913–1952 [with André Parinaud] (1952). ENGLISH: *Conversations: The Autobiography of Surrealism,* trans. Mark Polizzotti. New York: Paragon House, 1993.

La Clé des champs (1953). ENGLISH: *Free Rein,* trans. Michel Parmentier and Jacqueline d'Amboise. Lincoln: University of Nebraska Press, 1995.

Constellations [with Joan Miró] (1959). ENGLISH: Paul Hammond, *Constellations of Miró, Breton.* San Francisco: City Lights Books, 2000.

Perspective cavalière [ed. Marguerite Bonnet] (1970).

ANTHOLOGIES OF BRETON'S
POETRY IN ENGLISH

Selected Poems, trans. Kenneth White. London: Jonathan Cape, 1969.

Poems of André Breton: A Bilingual Anthology, ed. and trans. Jean-Pierre Cauvin and Mary Ann Caws. Austin: University of Texas Press, 1982.

Earthlight, trans. Bill Zavatsky and Zack Rogow. Los Angeles: Sun & Moon Press, 1993. Includes selected poems from *Mont de Piété* through *L'Air de l'eau.*

My Heart Through Which Her Heart Has Passed: Poems of Love and Desperation, trans. Mark Polizzotti. Paris and London: Alyscamps Press, 1998. Uncollected love poems written between 1926 and 1931.

SEE ALSO:

The Poetry of Surrealism, ed. Michael Benedikt. Boston: Little, Brown and Co., 1974.

The Random House Book of Twentieth-Century French Poetry, ed. Paul Auster. New York: Random House, 1982.

WORKS ABOUT ANDRÉ BRETON
AND SURREALISM

Balakian, Anna. *André Breton: Magus of Surrealism.* New York: Oxford University Press, 1971.

Caws, Mary Ann. *André Breton.* New York: Twayne, 1973; revised ed., 1996.

————. *The Poetry of Dada and Surrealism: Aragon, Breton, Tzara, Eluard, and Desnos.* Princeton: Princeton University Press, 1971.

Eluard, Paul. *Letters to Gala,* trans. Jesse Browner. New York: Paragon House, 1989.

Gershman, Herbert. *The Surrealist Revolution in France.* Ann Arbor: University of Michigan Press, 1968.

Nadeau, Maurice. *The History of Surrealism,* trans. Richard Howard. Cambridge, Mass.: Harvard University Press, 1989.

Polizzotti, Mark. *Revolution of the Mind: The Life of André Breton.* New York: Farrar, Straus and Giroux, 1995.

Thirion, André. *Revolutionaries Without a Revolution,* trans. Joachim Neugroschel. New York: Macmillan, 1975.

OF RELATED INTEREST

Aragon, Louis. *Paris Peasant,* trans. Simon Watson Taylor. Boston: Exact Change, 1994.

Artaud, Antonin. *Selected Writings,* ed. Susan Sontag, trans. Helen Weaver. New York: Farrar, Straus and Giroux, 1976.

*4 Dada Suicides: Selected Texts of Arthur Cravan, Jacques Rigaut, Julien Torma &
Jacques Vaché.* London: Atlas Press, 1995. Includes the complete text of
Vaché's "war letters" to Breton.

Comte de Lautréamont. *Maldoror and the Complete Works,* trans. Alexis Lyki-
ard. Boston: Exact Change, 1994.

Levy, Julien, ed., *Surrealism.* New York: Da Capo Press, 1995. A facsimile
reprint of Levy's limited-edition 1936 anthology, offering a good overview of
Surrealism in its heyday.

Tzara, Tristan. *Seven Dada Manifestos and Lampisteries,* trans. Barbara Wright.
London: John Calder, 1977.

COPYEDITING:	CAROLINE ROBERTS AT WILSTED & TAYLOR PUBLISHING SERVICES
DESIGN AND COMPOSITION:	JEFF CLARK AT WILSTED & TAYLOR PUBLISHING SERVICES
TEXT:	GRANJON
DISPLAY:	AKZIDENZ GROTESQUE
PRINTER AND BINDER:	THOMSON-SHORE, INC.